LIVING A HEALTHY LIFESTYLE DOES NOT HAVE TO BE
DIFFICULT

HOW TO ACHIEVE OPTIMAL HEALTH THROUGH DIET AND LIFESTYLE CHANGES

SHIKA SIMPSON

Kravitz & Sons

INNOVATORS IN PUBLISHING MARKETING AND ADVERTISING

Kravitz and Sons LLC
1301 Farmville Blvd, Suite 104
Greenville, NC 27834

Published by Kravitz and Sons LLC.

ISBN: 979-8-89639-282-8 (sc)
ISBN: 979-8-89639-283-5 (e)

Library of Congress Control Number: 2025915017

Dedications

Dedicated to all my colleagues from The Institute for Integrative Nutrition, and The School of Applied Functional Medicine, who are making a big difference in people's lives as Health Coaches, Holistic Health, practitioners and Functional Medicine practitioners around the globe.

Thanks for all your contributions to healthcare and let us continue to change lives in all that we do.

Table Of Contents

CHAPTER 6

CHAPTER 10

Slow Down The Ageing Process!   **146**

Introduction

Congratulations on making the effort to lead a healthier lifestyle! That you are reading this book means you are ready for a change and I'm so glad you made that decision.

Welcome aboard!

As an Integrative Nutrition Health Coach, a Holistic Health Consultant, and a Functional Medicine student, it breaks my heart to see my clients struggling with chronic lifestyle diseases like type 2 diabetes for instance, which could have simply been avoided or even reversed, by making long-term sustainable lifestyle changes.

Driven by my passion for health and wellness, I decided to write this book to educate, guide, and empower people to make the necessary, sustainable lifestyle changes and to take control of their own health in order to enjoy life to the fullest and to be free of health challenges, especially as they grow older.

You may have read lots of contradictory articles about nutrition, health, and wellness and are probably confused. You may be trying so hard to make the necessary lifestyle changes but are so overwhelmed with all the confusing information out there that you just don't know where to begin. In that case, just put all those conflicting ideas to rest, and let's make a fresh start.

I invite you to come with me as we embark on this health and wellness journey starting today, in order to transform your life and live a healthier lifestyle.

We shall look at the main causes of health issues and how to give the body what it needs to thrive, heal, and prevent further health struggles.

From the pages of this book, I hope you will discover fun and interesting ways of learning that living a **healthy lifestyle** does not need to be difficult or expensive at all!

Chapter 1

Food Is Medicine!

"When diet is WRONG, Medicine is of NO USE.
When diet is CORRECT, Medicine is of NO NEED."

— Famous Ayurvedic saying

The foods and beverages we consume profoundly affect our health. It is therefore crucial to provide the body with the right combination of nutrients necessary for building and repairing tissues, boosting the immune system to fight infections, and supplying energy for day-to-day activities in order to thrive.

Chronic diseases such as heart disease, diabetes, high blood pressure, bone loss, obesity, and certain cancers, all have a connection to poor diets and could be prevented with proper nutrition and other lifestyle changes. Though all the above-mentioned diseases could be inherited because they run in certain families, inheriting bad genes doesn't mean that one should end up with diseases. Those bad genes could be turned off by nourishing the body with a proper diet and by making all the necessary lifestyle changes.

To adopt a diet that supports growth, prevents diseases, and promotes healing, it's essential to know which foods to consume and which ones to avoid, as well as how to combine them for proper nourishment of the body.

Essential Nutrients

A healthy diet should provide all the necessary nutrients required for muscle growth and development, as well as fight infections.

The three main essential nutrients the body needs to function properly are carbohydrates, proteins, fats, plus water. These are collectively known as *macronutrients*. "Macro" means large, as these nutrients are required in substantial amounts for the body's optimal functioning.

— Carbohydrates

These are sugar molecules bonded together with carbon, hydrogen, and oxygen. Sugar, starch, and fibre are all carbohydrates. They provide and store energy.

There are two types of carbohydrates:

1. Simple carbohydrates, made up of just one or two sugar molecules. They are easily absorbed into the bloodstream but have no nutritional value.

Examples are table sugar, candy, soft drinks, fruit juices, jams, syrups, pastries, and refined grain cereals. Milk and milk products contain lactose, a simple sugar, but contain smaller amounts of carbohydrates.

2. Complex carbohydrates on the other hand, are made up of more sugar molecules bonded together. They are mostly plant foods, fibre, and starches. They are rich in vitamins, minerals, and antioxidants. Due to their high fibre content, they are slow to digest, more satisfying, and promote regularity and good health in general.

Examples of complex carbohydrates are whole grains; brown rice, quinoa, millet, fruits, green vegetables, sweet potatoes, beans, lentils, peas, etc.

- Carbohydrates are the body's preferred food source for energy. They are broken down into glucose, which all the cells and tissues in our body use for energy. The central nervous system, the brain, the kidneys, the heart, and other muscles all need it in order to function properly.

- Simple carbohydrates cause blood sugar to rise quickly and can lead to weight gain and diabetes if the levels remain chronically high, especially for overweight people.

For instance, when hunger strikes and you reach out for a candy bar, pastry, or any other simple carbohydrate, it will be easily absorbed into the bloodstream without providing a sense of satiety. Consequently, there's a tendency to consume more in order to feel full. This results in blood sugar spikes, which over time, will gradually progress to pre-diabetes and eventually type 2 diabetes if the pattern continues. To prevent this, it is advisable to avoid refined carbohydrates and focus on eating whole grains and vegetables instead. These will leave you feeling full because they take longer to digest without raising blood sugar levels.

- Combining carbohydrates with vegetables, proteins, and healthy fats will slow down digestion and lower its impact on blood sugar levels.

- Replacing refined carbohydrates like white bread, white pasta, cereal, and white flour baked goods with complex carbohydrates like vegetables, fruits, whole grains, nuts, and seeds will promote stable blood sugar levels. Whole grains should be pre-soaked before cooking to soften the grains for easy digestion.

- The Institute of Medicine recommends that 45 to 65% of total calories consumed by adults daily should be from carbohydrates.

- The total calories consumed daily depend on age, gender, and activity level. For instance, if your daily calorie intake is between 1500 and 2000, then you should be consuming 675 to 975 or 900 to 1300 calories in carbohydrates, respectively.

- Dark leafy greens should form part of the daily carbohydrate intake as they are rich in vitamins, minerals, antioxidants, phytonutrients, and fibre.
  i. They are essential for maintaining a healthy immune system.
  ii. They are high in alkaline and therefore, beneficial for exposure to toxins since the alkaline minerals in the body neutralise the acidic conditions brought about by environmental toxins.
  iii. They help prevent cancer.
  iv. Certain leafy greens like spinach, beet greens, and Swiss chard are high in oxalic acid, which prevents the absorption of calcium. They should, therefore, be consumed in moderation.
  v. My recommendation is to have at least two cups of greens with every meal in order to crowd out junk food and maintain stable blood sugar levels.
  vi. I recommend choosing organic leafy greens but, it is better to eat inorganic than not eat any greens at all.

— Fibre

Fibre refers to types of carbohydrates that cannot be digested by the body. They pass through the intestinal tract and move waste out of the body.

There are two types of fibre:

1. **Soluble fibre:** This soaks up water as it passes through the system and turns into a gel. This slows down digestion, enabling the body to absorb nutrients slowly. Examples are beans, peas, lentils, apples, citrus fruits, avocado, broccoli, Brussels

sprouts, sweet potatoes, oat bran, nuts, and seeds (chia, psyllium, ground flax seeds).

2. **Insoluble fibre:** This adds bulk to the stools and speeds up the rate at which stool moves through the intestines for easy elimination, keeping the digestive tract clean. Examples are flaxseeds, wheat bran, whole grains, etc.

- Inadequate fibre in the diet causes constipation, haemorrhoids, *irritable bowel syndrome* IBS, and *diverticulitis*, increasing the risk for colon and bowel cancers.
- On the other hand, a diet rich in fibre promotes regularity, helps lower cholesterol, and decreases the risk for obesity and heart disease.

— Proteins

Proteins are the most important of the macronutrients. They form the building blocks of the body. They are broken down into twenty amino acids, out of which nine are essential, which means the body does not make them. Since amino acids are not stored, it is important to have some protein every day.

- Proteins are needed for growth, especially in children, teens, and pregnant women.
- They build and repair body tissues.
- They produce antibodies for the immune system.
- They maximise the transportation of oxygen to tissues.
- They manufacture essential hormones and enzymes.
- They help build and repair muscles after workouts.
- They help to preserve lean muscle mass.
- They provide energy when carbohydrates are not available.

- Proteins are found in meats and fish, poultry, cheese, milk, legumes, nuts, and in very small quantities in some vegetables and grains.
- Proteins from animal sources contain all the essential amino acids, whereas plant sources of protein do not.
- The richest sources of proteins include animal products like meat, dairy, eggs, and fish.
- Plant sources include beans, nuts, and seeds.

Careful consideration should be given to selecting animal protein sources. When purchasing fresh animal products, check the dates and consider the animal's upbringing and slaughter methods. Look for the 'Certified Humane' logo, which ensures that the animal was allowed to behave naturally from birth until slaughter, with standards of slaughter to minimise pain during the process. Always choose pasture-raised, hormone-free, antibiotic-free, grass-fed, or organic beef, as well as organic or pasture-raised chicken and pasture-raised, organic, or omega-3 whole eggs. The same applies to duck, turkey, and other domestic fowls.

Processed meats: These are meats preserved by curing, smoking, salting, drying, or using harmful chemical additives like nitrates, nitrites, sodium benzoate, and more. These additives increase the formation of carcinogens, such meats should therefore be avoided.

Examples of processed meats include sausages, salami, pepperoni, hot dogs, smoked meats, ham, cured bacon, beef jerky, corned beef, luncheon meat, and other canned meats.

With regard to plant proteins, avoid fake meats, which are meat substitutes like textured vegetable protein (TVP), for instance. It is made from soy with the addition of other ingredients like wheat, oats, or cottonseed. Soy is genetically modified and a known *allergen*. (Can cause an allergic reaction) The same goes for plant-based burgers, soy yoghurt, and other animal product substitutes made from soy. Secondly, these are processed foods. It is better to eat whole foods, foods made from scratch at home, using wholesome ingredients, rather than foods made at a processing plant.

Remember, if it comes in a can, box, or plastic container, it's processed and best avoided. This point is emphasised by Michael Pollan in "The Omnivore's Dilemma": "Don't eat anything that your great-great-grandmother wouldn't recognise as food." (Referring to processed foods)

Fish and seafood are also excellent sources of protein and are rich in omega-3 fatty acids, which are essential for a healthy heart and brain. Examples include sardines, mackerel, salmon, trout, and halibut.

Always choose wild-caught fish and seafood over factory-farmed varieties, as farmed fish often contain higher levels of pollutants like chlorinated pesticides, dioxins, and methylmercury. Note also that certain fish and shellfish, such as swordfish, shark, tuna, and other large species, may have higher mercury levels and should be consumed less frequently. It is better to choose smaller fish instead with lower mercury levels, such as anchovies, clams, oysters, scallops, shrimp, squid, and tilapia, as recommended by the Food and Drug Administration (FDA).

Pregnant women and young children should avoid fish with elevated mercury levels.

The Institute of Medicine recommends that 10 to 35% of our daily calorie intake should come from proteins. Use this guideline to ensure you're meeting your daily protein requirements.

— Fats

Despite their bad reputation for causing weight gain, dietary fats are essential macronutrients necessary for survival. The body requires a certain amount of essential fatty acids, but these cannot be made internally and must be obtained through food. There are two fatty acids, omega-3 and omega-6 essential for humans.

There are three main omega-3 fatty acids, namely *alpha-linolenic acid* (ALA), *eicosapentaenoic acid* (EPA), and *docosahexaenoic acid* (DHA). ALA is found mostly in plants such as flaxseed, walnuts, and hemp seeds, while EPA and DHA are found in fish, seafood, seaweed, and algae.

Omega-3 fatty acids possess anti-inflammatory properties and may help lower the risk of chronic diseases such as heart disease, cancer, and arthritis. Linolenic acid (LA), on the other hand, is an omega-6 fatty acid primarily found in seeds and seed oils. They are *pro-inflammatory*, which means diets high in omega-6 promote inflammation.

- The main role of fatty acids is to help control inflammation.
- They also help control blood clotting and the development of the brain.
- They regulate the production of hormones.
- They help the body absorb fat-soluble vitamins like A, D, E, and K.
- They maintain cell membranes.
- They are stored in fat cells to insulate the body and keep it warm.

There are 3 types of dietary fats as follows:

1. Saturated fats; found mostly in animal products like butter, ghee, lard, suet, cheese, whole milk, cream, and fatty meats.
    - Vegetable oils such as coconut, palm, and palm kernel oils also contain saturated fats.

- Beef, lamb, and pork are also high in saturated fats.
- Saturated fats are solid at room temperature.

2. Unsaturated fats can be *monounsaturated* or *polyunsaturated*.

   o Monounsaturated fats contain one unsaturated chemical bond. Olive, avocado, and almond oils are all examples of monounsaturated fats. They are liquid at room temperature. Monounsaturated fats lower LDL or bad cholesterol.

   o Polyunsaturated fats have more than one unsaturated chemical bond. Sunflower, corn, and soybean oils are all polyunsaturated fats. These oils are refined, over-processed, and pro-inflammatory and, therefore, not recommended.

3. Trans-fats or partially hydrogenated fats are vegetable oils infused with hydrogen to produce a semi-solid fat to keep food fresh for a long time and prolong shelf life. Margarine and shortening are trans-fats. Trans-fats can be found in commercially baked goods, fried foods such as doughnuts, French fries, fried chicken, frozen pizza, refrigerated dough for biscuits and rolls, microwave popcorn, and non-dairy coffee creamers.

   Trans-fats increase the risk for heart disease by raising LDL cholesterol, which is the bad cholesterol and should be avoided at all costs.

   - Choosing unsaturated fats like extra virgin olive oil, avocado oil, avocados, olives, and nuts over saturated and trans-fats decreases the risk for heart disease.
   - Trans fats have been banned by the FDA since 2018 and are no longer found on the list of ingredients on food labels. However, when dining out, it is difficult to know which foods still have trans-fats, so to be on the safer side, it is best to avoid commercially fried foods and baked goods altogether.

Only use pure, organic, cold-pressed, unrefined oils as refined oils are altered using chemicals and therefore unhealthy. Examples of refined oils to avoid are vegetable, sunflower, soybean, corn, safflower, grape seed, and canola oils. These oils are processed using very high heat and toxic chemicals as well as bleached and deodorised.

- **Olive oil** has a low smoke point and should not be used in frying or any cooking that requires very high temperatures. When olive oil is heated beyond its smoke point, its health benefits are destroyed, and it releases toxic fumes instead. It should only be used for low-heat or no-heat cooking, for salad dressings, or as a condiment.

  My recommendation is to avoid frying food altogether. However, if you have to fry, do not use olive oil. Use avocado or coconut oil instead.

- **Almond oil:** Unrefined, cold-pressed, almond oil contains monounsaturated fats and vitamin E. It supports heart health and helps to reduce LDL cholesterol. It can be used in cooking and on hair and skin. However, unrefined almond oil is not stable under high temperatures and is best used for low-heat or no-heat food preparation.

- **Hazelnut oil:** Unrefined, cold-pressed, hazelnut oil is another healthy fat. It is rich in monounsaturated fatty acids, vitamins, and minerals. It is a very good anti-inflammatory due to its richness in antioxidants. It is able to withstand medium to high temperatures and, therefore, ideal for sautéing, grilling, and baking, as well as in vinaigrettes or salad dressings.

  - According to the Dietary Intake reference published by the US Department of Agriculture, USDA 20 to 35% of our total daily calorie intake should come from fats.

— Water

In addition to the above-mentioned essential nutrients, water is also considered a macronutrient since it is needed in large quantities in order for our bodies to survive.

- The average person's body is made up of about 60-70% water.

- Unlike carbohydrates, proteins, and fats, water contains zero calories and therefore does not provide any energy.

- Water is needed to deliver oxygen and nutrients throughout the body; without it cells will die.

- Water is also needed for absorption, digestion, circulation, and excretion.

- Water flushes out toxin-build up from the body.

- It is important to replace water lost through body fluids by drinking lots of water.

- Caffeine acts as a *diuretic*; it increases the output of urine. People who consume caffeinated beverages should, therefore, drink more and more water.

- Drink water even when you are not thirsty!

- Inadequate consumption of water results in excess body fat, digestive problems, constipation, and poor functioning of the organs.

- Drinking water should be free from contaminants like pesticides, heavy metals, and other harmful chemicals that the body does not need.

- Daily recommended intakes: Men 3.5 litres, women 3 litres.

- Start your day with two cups (500 ml) of water before drinking or eating anything.

— Micronutrients

These are the nutrients required in smaller quantities but are nonetheless crucial for the development of the human body. There are two types; vitamins and minerals.

Vitamins fall into two categories; water-soluble and fat-soluble. A balanced diet should typically supply an adequate amount of these micronutrients. Failure to get the recommended amount can prevent muscle growth and increase susceptibility to infections and diseases.

- Water-soluble vitamins are the B-complex vitamins and vitamin C. These are easily excreted in the urine and must be supplemented regularly.
- Fat-soluble vitamins, on the other hand, are A, D, E, and K. These do not need to be replaced regularly because, unlike water-soluble vitamins, they are stored in the liver, fatty tissue, and muscles. They are easily absorbed by the body with the help of dietary fats.

Vitamin A

- Functions:
  - It helps with good eyesight and prevents night blindness.
  - It helps improve the immune system.
  - It helps to slow down the ageing process.
  - Regular increased intake can result in toxic levels.
  - It helps to lower cholesterol and reduce the risk of heart disease and stroke.
  - It helps with the growth of bones and the normal development of body cells.
  - Daily recommended intakes: 900 mcg for men, 700 mcg for women.
  - A deficiency could result in night blindness and blindness.

- Good Sources:
    - Milk
    - Beef liver
    - Leafy greens, yellow and orange vegetables (spinach, bell peppers, carrot).

Vitamin D

- Functions:
    - It functions as a hormone.
    - It maintains good, strong bones and teeth.
    - It enhances the immune system.
    - A deficiency can result in high blood pressure, some cancers, and abnormal bone growth.
    - Daily recommended intakes: IU (international units) minimum 1000-2000 IU maximum.

- Good Sources:
    - Sunlight
    - Salmon
    - Fish oil, Shrimp
    - Dairy products

Vitamin E

- Functions:
    - It is an *antioxidant*, which means it protects the body from *oxidation* (damage caused by exposure to oxygen).

- It provides protection to all body cells.

- It prevents diabetes and cancer.

- It protects against heart disease.

- A weakened immune system and vision problems may be signs of a vitamin E deficiency.

- Recommended daily intakes: 15 milligrams or 22 IU (international units).

- Good Sources:
  - Wheat germ
  - Nuts and seeds
  - Beet greens, collard greens, spinach
  - Peanut, peanut butter

Vitamin K

- Functions:
  - It helps with the production of proteins that are necessary for blood to clot to enable cuts and wounds to stop bleeding.
  - It is responsible for normal bone formation.
  - It converts glucose to glycogen for storage.
  - It helps to prevent arterial hardening.
  - It lowers the risk for diabetes.
  - It helps fight cancer.
  - It prevents heart disease.
  - Recommended daily intakes: Men 120 mcg, women 90 mcg

- Good sources:
    - Kale
    - Cabbage
    - Cauliflower
    - Broccoli, Brussels sprouts
    - Spinach, collard greens

Vitamin B Complex

There are eight B vitamins that make up the B complex. They all work together and contribute to the overall functioning of the body.

- B-1 Thiamine
- B-2 Riboflavin
- B-3 Niacin
- B-5 Pantothenic acid
- B-6 Pyridoxine
- B-7 Biotin
- B-9 Folic acid
- B-12 Cobalamin
    - B Vitamins are needed for the breakdown of carbohydrates into glucose.
    - They also help with the breakdown of fats and proteins.
    - Sources include meat, dark green vegetables, and grains.
    - Vegans are at risk for pernicious anaemia, a B12 deficiency, and will need to take supplements.

Vitamin C

Vitamin C performs a variety of functions in the body.

- o It helps to absorb iron. It maintains the connective tissues and also acts as an antioxidant.
- o It is available in most fruits and vegetables.
- o Using tobacco depletes the body's vitamin C. Smokers and those who chew tobacco will, therefore, need more vitamin C than others.
- o Vitamin C deficiencies include scurvy, the inability of wounds to heal, and frequent infections.
- o Recommended daily intakes: 1000 to 2000 mg.

- Good sources
  - o Found abundantly in fruits and vegetables
  - o Citrus fruits, such as oranges, and orange juice
  - o Peppers
  - o Strawberries, blackcurrants,
  - o Brussels sprouts, broccoli
  - o Potatoes

— Minerals

There are two major essential minerals; *macrominerals* and *microminerals.* Macrominerals are needed in larger amounts and are:

- Calcium
- Magnesium
- Phosphorus

- Sodium
- Potassium
- Chloride
- Sulphur

Microminerals are only needed in trace amounts. They are:

- Iron
- Copper
- Iodine
- Fluoride
- Manganese
- Cobalt
- Selenium
- Zinc
  - Minerals are found in plants and animals.
  - They are found in the soil and are absorbed by the plants.
  - Eating a healthy diet will enable you to get the right amount of minerals the body needs.
  - If you are taking medication, you may need less of some minerals. Ask your physician.

Probiotics: These are the friendly bacteria found in the digestive tract. A good balance of friendly and unfriendly bacteria is important for proper digestion and absorption of nutrients.

  - Probiotics are therefore essential for digestion, the production of some vitamins, for example, B12, and for the absorption of nutrients.

- o They help to reduce gas, bloating, and upset stomach.

- o They defend against pathogen colonisation in the digestive system.

- o They reduce the risk of infections.

- • Sources:

Probiotic-rich foods are fermented, and grow healthy bacterial cultures in the process. Yoghurt, kefir, sauerkraut, kombucha, and kimchi are all probiotic-rich foods. Additionally, miso, tempeh, and natto are also probiotic-rich foods made from fermented soybeans.

Beware of commercially prepared probiotic foods, as they may undergo pasteurisation. Pasteurisation kills harmful bacteria in food and will kill the friendly bacteria in probiotics as well.

Where Does Your Produce Come From?

To ensure that you get the most nutrients from your produce, it should come to you very fresh, ideally locally grown and harvested just in time for sale. This can only be made possible by buying from local farmers or farmers' markets within the community. Get to know the farmers, talk to them, and find out what practices are used to grow and harvest the crops. Do they use Roundup or other glyphosate-containing herbicides, or are they relying solely on organic weed killers and pesticides? Are any of the crops genetically modified?

Buying locally grown crops will ensure that the produce is fresh, has more nutrients, tastes better, and is less likely to be old and contaminated. Produce that comes from distant locations, or has been imported, needs to travel for a long time to get to the stores and probably takes time to be sorted before being displayed for sale. This encourages spoilage, contamination, and loss of nutrients, as well as loss of taste and flavour. Support the local farmers by buying locally grown produce.

The herbicides and pesticides utilised to safeguard crops and boost yields for greater profits often contain toxic chemicals detrimental to our health. Despite claims by Monsanto, (company that makes Roundup), of its safety for human use, studies have linked Roundup to cancer. The World Health Organization's Agency for International Research on Cancer reported findings of internal organ tumours in animals treated with glyphosate, thus establishing a connection between the chemical and cancer. Alarmingly, it has not been prohibited and continues to find its way into our food supply.

Contrarily, the Environmental Protection Agency (EPA) maintains that glyphosate poses no threat to human health, endorsing its use in genetically modified crops like soybeans, corn, and wheat. What exactly is a *Genetically Modified Organism* (GMO)? It's a plant or animal whose DNA has been altered using genetic engineering techniques to enhance resistance to pests, diseases, or environmental conditions. Currently, there are eleven recognised genetically modified crops including; corn, soybeans, cotton, potatoes, papayas, summer squash, apples, sugar beets, eggplants, canola, and alfalfa. Awareness of which foods are genetically modified helps us know what foods to buy and which ones to avoid.

Identifying GMO foods however, isn't straightforward as they aren't labelled. Some hidden sources of GM foods include dietary supplements such as vitamins C, E, B2, B12, and biotin, as well as fructose, aspartame, baking powder, beta carotene, soy sauce, soy lecithin, textured vegetable protein, maltodextrin, whey, and xanthan gum.

While pesticides and herbicides aren't directly applied to animals, they are used on the corn, wheat, and soy fed to livestock, allowing these chemicals to get into the skin as well as the meat of the animals.

Consider Buying Organic Produce And Meat

Organic farming does not involve the use of synthetic pesticides or chemicals that could contaminate groundwater or harm wildlife, making it an environmentally safe practice. Additionally, organic farming prohibits the use of growth hormones, antibiotics on farm animals, and arsenic in chicken feed, and the animals are pasture-raised.

Choosing organic produce is the best way to eliminate the harmful effects of pesticides on your health. Food that is grown without pesticides offers the healthiest diet, ensuring your body receives optimal nourishment.

Organic produce is becoming more and more popular despite the fact that it costs more than conventionally grown. It is better to pay a bit more for high-quality food and have less exposure to the toxic chemicals that end up in food. All organic agricultural farms must adhere to stringent guidelines verified by the USDA-approved independent agency.

Organic produce provides an increased intake of *polyphenols* (micronutrients found naturally in plants that act as antioxidants, protecting against oxidative stress). These compounds, including vitamins C and E, may lower the risk of cardiovascular and neurodegenerative diseases, lower blood sugar levels, improve digestion, and protect against certain cancers.

According to a study conducted by the Environmental Working Group (EWG), approximately 63% of conventionally grown fruits and vegetables retain pesticide residue even after being thoroughly washed. The EWG, an American activist group specialising in research and advocacy regarding toxic chemicals, drinking water pollutants, and agricultural subsidies, releases lists of the most contaminated and least contaminated produce every year. Check their website, *www.ewg.org*, for updates on the 'Dirty Dozen' and 'Clean Fifteen' each year.

Here is the current list of the EWG's Dirty Dozen (most contaminated produce):

1. Strawberries
2. Spinach
3. Kale, collard, and mustard greens
4. Nectarines
5. Apples
6. Grapes
7. Cherries
8. Peaches
9. Pears
10. Bell and hot peppers
11. Celery
12. Tomatoes

Clean Fifteen (fruits and vegetables with the lowest traces of pesticides):

1. Avocados
2. Sweet corn
3. Pineapple
4. Onions
5. Papaya
6. Sweet peas
7. Eggplant
8. Asparagus

9. Broccoli

10. Cabbage

11. Kiwi

12. Cauliflower

13. Mushrooms

14. Honeydew melon

15. Cantaloupe

To save money on organic produce, consider growing your own basic vegetables and fruits. You could join community gardens located in every city, or buy planter boxes and organic soil from hardware stores. If you live in an apartment and have a balcony, you can still grow tomatoes, peppers, and leafy greens in pots during spring. Perennials like strawberries, raspberries, and blueberries don't require annual replanting; you can plant them in the spring and don't need to replant them ever again.

If you cannot grow your own produce and can't afford to buy organic then use the Dirty Dozen and Clean Fifteen as a guide when buying produce.

Price Look-Up Codes

To distinguish between organic and inorganic produce, examine the price look-up code on individual fruits and vegetables. Conventionally grown items typically have a 4-digit code beginning with #4. For instance, a little sticker marked #4011 indicates an inorganic yellow banana. Organic produce, on the other hand, features a 5-digit code beginning with #9; for example, #94011 signifies an organic yellow banana. Genetically modified produce is also identified by a 5-digit code starting with #8; for instance, #84011 indicates a genetically modified yellow banana.

Let's Go Grocery Shopping

Below is a table of a list of clean grocery items you need in your fridge and pantry just to give you an idea of what to put in your shopping cart.

Vegetables	Fruit	Herbs & Spices	Condiments	Protein	Nuts, Seeds & Oils
Carrots	Apples	Basil Cinnamon	Apple cider vinegar	Beef	Almonds
Garlic	Avocado	Cayenne pepper	Balsamic vinegar	Chicken	Cashews
Leafy greens	Bananas	Chilli flakes	Hot sauce	Eggs	Chia seeds
Onions	Berries	Ginger	Pure maple syrup	Fish	Coconut oil
Peppers	Grapefruit	Oregano	Raw honey	Green peas	Flax seeds
Squash	Lemons	Parsley	Salsa	Lentils	Nut butters
Sweet Potatoes	Oranges	Black Pepper	Sea salt	Tempeh	Olive oil
	Pears	Turmeric	Soy or tamarind sauce	Tofu	Pistachios
				Turkey	

Food Preparation

The food we consume should be as close to what nature intended it to be as possible, without any processing and additives. However, not all foods can be eaten raw. Some foods require some cooking to make them safe for consumption. There is also the need to add seasoning, herbs, and spices to make food more palatable.

- The foods that could be eaten raw should be eaten raw in order not to destroy the vital nutrients they contain.

- Do not overcook food, as nutrients tend to escape by getting destroyed by heat or being dissolved in the cooking water. Water in which vegetables are cooked could be saved as vegetable stock for soups.

- Avoid deep fat frying and grilling as much as possible. When meat is grilled, the fat drips into the flame, causing the formation of compounds known as *advanced glycation end products* (AGEs), which can promote *carcinogenesis*, the beginning of cancer formation. Additionally roasting, broiling, and toasting could also cause the formation of AGEs. Avoid all charred foods in general, as they are potential carcinogens. Fried foods are harder to digest, especially in the case of people with low stomach acid, low bile production, and low digestive juices, thus causing upset stomach, indigestion, and heartburn.

- Use only fresh or frozen produce. Avoid canned vegetables and fruits as they contain too much sodium, added sugars, preservatives, and other additives.

- Always read the ingredients list on food labels and avoid foods with hard-to-pronounce ingredients which most probably are chemical additives. The body finds it hard to digest such additives.

- Avoid using stock cubes, powders, or any other flavour enhancers, as these contain *monosodium glutamate*, MSG, a chemical additive known to cause health problems.

How Safe Is Your Cookware?

In addition to cooking in a hygienic manner, using clean utensils, and preparing fresh foods in a clean environment, the type of utensils used in food preparation and storage, are just as important as the food itself for optimal health. Certain heavy metals found in cookware can produce toxic reactions upon contact with food, and this could negatively impact both the food and our health.

- **Aluminium:** Aluminium is a heavy metal. It is considered to be a *neurotoxin*, poisonous to the nervous system. When heated, it can react with acidic foods, causing it to gradually leach into the food and can cause stomach upsets and other health issues. It is even linked to *Alzheimer's* disease and *Lou Gehrig's disease.* (ALS) Although the World Health Organization claims that it is safe for adults to ingest more than 50 milligrams of aluminium daily, constant exposure and excess amounts of every heavy metal can lead to heavy metal poisoning. Since there is a trace of aluminium everywhere; in our water, in foods, drugs, and cosmetics, exposure to lethal amounts should be limited by not allowing it to leach into food through the constant use of aluminium cooking pots and foil.

- **Teflon:** This is a chemical coating known as *polytetrafluoroethylene* (PTFE) used in non-stick pots, pans, and bakeware. It is not recommended for cooking at high temperatures as it releases toxic gases and chemicals when heated. It is only good to use for medium to low temperatures. The empty pot should not be heated dry as this could cause toxic particles to be released into the atmosphere. Do have some oil or liquid in a Teflon-coated pan before it gets heated. Avoid using metal utensils with Teflon-coated pans in order not to scratch the coating and release the Teflon particles into food. Scratched Teflon-coated pots should no longer be used to avoid releasing toxic chemicals into food.

Perfluorooctanoic acid (PFOA) is another chemical found in Teflon cookware. Even though there are claims that it is only in small amounts, like all other hidden toxins, PFOA is everywhere in the environment, on fabrics, and personal care products, and it is best to limit our exposure as much as possible by avoiding this cookware altogether, especially as it becomes old and scratched. PFOA has been classified by the International Agency for Research on Cancer (IARC) as possibly carcinogenic.

- **Copper:** This metal is a very good conductor of heat and quickly and evenly heats up making it ideal for cooking. However, cooking with copper can be toxic. Copper reacts with acidic foods; uncoated copper can therefore leach into food when cooking acidic foods, and can cause diarrhoea, nausea and vomiting. On the other hand, when coated, the coating may contain nickel, another heavy metal, which can also cause heavy metal poisoning when exposed to larger amounts.

- **Ceramic-coated cookware** is easy to cook with and to clean because it has a non-stick coating. However, it is not durable as the coating starts chipping with time, causing food to be exposed to lead, cadmium, or both, which may be present in the coating. To be on the safer side, it is best to avoid using this cookware once chipping starts since exposure to either of these heavy metals in large amounts can cause heavy metal poisoning and certain types of cancers.

Safer Cookware Options

The material used in manufacturing the cookware and the coating layer determines its safety. It is, therefore, essential that the inner coating of the cookware be non-toxic to ensure that food is cooked safely without any toxic chemicals leaching into it.

- **Pyrex:** This is a heat and chemical-resistant glass that can be used as a mixing bowl, for cooking, baking, reheating, and storing food. It is considered to be safe for cooking since it does not give out toxic fumes or leach any chemicals into food. Most Pyrex containers however, have plastic lids, which brings to mind *Bisphenol-A* (BPA), an industrial chemical used in making certain plastic containers, water bottles, and line cans in canned food production. Some research shows that PBA could seep into beverages or food. BPA is an *endocrine disruptor*, a chemical compound that interferes with the normal functioning of the endocrine system. This disruption can lead to infertility, birth defects, and cancerous tumours. According to the Environmental Working Group, The Can Manufacturers Institute has phased out the use of BPA, and today about 95 % of food cans are made without BPA linings. The BPA has been replaced with other coatings or polymers.

Most plastic containers nowadays are labelled BPA-free, yet little is known about the toxicity of the coatings replacing BPA. It's advisable to refrain from heating food in plastic containers in the microwave. If using glass bowls for microwave heating, avoid covering the food with its lid, or any plastic or saran wrap (cling film). While the USDA maintains that microwave-safe saran wrap is safe for use, it's important to note that saran wrap is *thermoplastic*, melts when heated causing chemicals to leach into food. Care should be taken not to overheat, when using it in the microwave. Ideally, it's best to avoid using plastic altogether in the microwave, as heating may cause chemicals to leach into foods.

Additionally, *expanded polystyrene* foam, (EPS) also known as Styrofoam, deserves to be mentioned. Styrofoam contains styrene and benzene, both neurotoxins and possible carcinogens, which could leach into warm food or beverages and be absorbed into the bloodstream and tissues. Styrofoam has been banned in most countries and even certain cities in the US due to health and environmental concerns. It is not biodegradable and harmful to the environment as well. Avoid it at all costs!

- **Cast iron:** This cookware is heavy and takes longer to heat, but it does not leach any toxic chemicals into food. It may help people who are iron deficient as it is believed that some of the iron will get into the food during cooking. Care must be taken to prevent it from rusting. Do not soak for extended periods. Do not wash with soap. Dry and rub with oil to season after use, then place on low heat for about an hour.

- **Enamel-covered cast iron:** This is also a very safe cookware as it is non-toxic and does not react with any food

- **100% Ceramic:** Ceramic cookware is quite heavy, but it is a good conductor of heat and durable. It can be used on the stove top as well as in the oven and even the fridge. It is non-toxic, does not leach into food, and does not chip or scratch.

- **Stainless steel:** Food-grade stainless steel is another safe cookware. It does not react with acidic foods and will not leach any toxic chemicals into food. Meyer Select is the only brand that I use because it is 100% nickel-free and durable too.

Foods To Be Wary Of

A healthy diet provides a balance of carbohydrates, protein, fibre, healthy fats, vitamins, and minerals. Certain foods, however, are not as healthy as they may seem to be and are likely to cause health issues for certain individuals. For instance, dairy products; such as milk, cheese, yoghurt, and butter.

— Dairy

Despite the government encouraging children and even adults to drink milk daily for strong bones, it's important to note that cow's milk is intended for calves, not humans. Consequently, consuming milk may potentially do more harm than good.

- Milk and dairy products are *pro-inflammatory*, promoting inflammation and potentially causing respiratory diseases, allergies, acne, eczema, and even cancer.

- Most people are *lactose intolerant* (unable to digest lactose, the sugar found in milk), which can lead to bloating, gas, and other gastrointestinal disorders.

- Additionally, 80% of milk is *casein*, the protein found in milk. It is pro-inflammatory and likely to trigger inflammation, leading to skin rashes, acne, and sinus congestion.

- So far, there's no evidence suggesting that drinking milk prevents osteoporosis and fractures, since countries where far less milk is consumed have lower rates of osteoporosis and hip fractures compared to the US, which consumes a higher amount. There are better and richer sources of calcium and all other nutrients in cow's milk.

- Excessive calcium intake can do more harm than good as it increases the risk of high calcium levels in the blood, potentially leading to kidney stones, high blood pressure, and an increased risk of heart attacks. Hence, it is not necessary for adults to consume cow's milk with every meal.

- While cheese may provide calcium essential for strong bones and healthy teeth, it may not be a healthy option after all. The saturated fat in cheese can elevate LDL (bad) cholesterol levels, increasing the risk for heart disease. Additionally, cheese contains high levels of sodium, which can raise blood pressure levels if consumed in excess. It may also cause discomfort for lactose-intolerant individuals, leading to gas, bloating, and an upset stomach. Finally, consuming too much-saturated fat from cheese could lead to weight gain and metabolic disorders.

- Yoghurt and milk kefir, however, are fermented and contain lactobacillus acidophilus bacteria, which promotes the growth of beneficial bacteria in the gut. These bacteria produce lactase, an enzyme that breaks down lactose into lactic acid, allowing lactose-intolerant individuals to consume fermented dairy without issues. Fermented dairy therefore, is safe to be consumed by most individuals. Choose organic, full-fat, plain yoghurt, or kefir without added sugar, artificial sweeteners, or other additives. If desired, sweeten with berries or other fruits. Avoid fat-free and low-fat dairy products as they tend to contain more added sugar.

- Butter is an exception, as it is made from milk by separating solid fats from liquid fats. It only contains traces of lactose and is high in fat, making it safe for lactose-intolerant individuals. Organic, pasture-raised butter is a healthy saturated fat that should be consumed in moderation.

- Finally, the oestrogen and other hormones in dairy products, whether organic or inorganic, could act as endocrine disruptors and may increase the risk for certain cancers like breast, ovarian, and prostate. The probability of early puberty in children due to the hormone in dairy, *recombinant bovine growth hormone* (rBGH), a synthetic hormone used to increase milk production in cows, is also another factor to be considered in deciding whether or not to consume dairy products.

— Sweeteners and sugar substitutes

Sugar, honey, agave nectar, maple syrup, coconut sugar, high fructose corn syrup, anhydrous dextrose, cane crystals, evaporated cane juice, fruit nectars, glucose, rice syrup, malt syrup, maltose, and sucrose, are all names of sugars added to foods and beverages during processing.

- Sugar occurs naturally in fruits, vegetables, and dairy, but these foods also contain vitamins, minerals, and fibre that slow down sugar absorption by the body. Added sugar, on the other hand, does more harm than good.

- Sugar is pro-inflammatory; it promotes *cellular inflammation,* leading to high cholesterol, high triglycerides, high blood pressure, and Alzheimer's disease. Additionally, cancer cells thrive on sugar.

- It causes *leptin resistance.* Leptin, the hormone that tells the body to stop eating when one is full, becomes ineffective, resulting in overeating and weight gain.

- It increases the risk of type 2 diabetes by causing obesity, which may also increase the risk of cancer and heart disease.

- Sugar accelerates the ageing process due to inflammation. It causes the skin to lose elasticity and appear older. Ageing may be a natural process, but it could be brought on prematurely by eating a poor diet and also consuming too much added sugar.

- Pure, unpasteurised honey contains phytonutrients—beneficial substances found in plants that help prevent diseases and provide antioxidant properties. It acts as an antifungal and antibacterial, giving it immune-boosting benefits, plus it contains some vitamins and minerals. However, it still contains fructose, glucose, and sucrose and can cause blood sugar spikes if consumed in excessive amounts.

Artificial sweeteners are a mixture of chemicals to create a sweet taste. The most common ones are *aspartame* (Equal or NutraSweet), *saccharin* (Sweet 'n' Low, Twin Sugar, or Sweet Twin), *sucralose* (Splenda), and *acesulfame potassium* (Sunett). These are all FDA-approved food additives. These sweeteners may contain zero calories and are consumed by most people trying to lose weight. However, it is important not to be misled by the 'zero calories' claim on food labels. Regrettably, artificial sweeteners do not promote weight loss; rather, they contribute to weight gain.

Artificial sweeteners confuse the brain by providing a sweet taste without accompanying calories. Consequently, this stimulates an increased appetite and cravings for foods and beverages that contain such sweeteners, leading to overeating, weight gain, and obesity. Studies have linked beverages containing artificial sweeteners to a higher risk of diabetes. Moreover, these sweeteners may cause headaches and depression, with potential carcinogenic effects observed in animal studies. Additionally, they disrupt beneficial gut bacteria.

— Sugar alcohols

These are a blend of sugar and alcohol molecules. Erythritol, maltitol, mannitol, sorbitol, and xylitol are all common alcohol sugars. Erythritol and sorbitol occur naturally in fruits and vegetables, but the alcohol sugars used in food processing are industrially produced from other sugars. They can be found in chewing gum, ice cream, low-calorie candies, toothpaste, etc. They are lower in calories and do not cause blood sugar spikes because they are not absorbed into the bloodstream like sugar. They are recognised as safe by the FDA. However, they may cause gas, bloating, diarrhoea, and other digestive issues because they cannot be fully digested by the body. When consumed in excess, they can still lead to weight gain.

Maltodextrin, a refined, processed carbohydrate, uses starch from rice, potato, corn, or wheat. It has no nutritional value and can cause blood sugar spikes. It is found in cereals, sports drinks, sauces, and baked goods.

Consuming excessive amounts of foods containing maltodextrin may result in weight gain and high cholesterol, leading to type 2 diabetes. It may also decrease the number of beneficial gut bacteria while increasing the bad bacteria. Additionally, it may contain gluten, making it unsuitable for individuals with celiac disease.

— Refined oils

These oils undergo processing with harmful chemicals like *hexane* and other solvents. Examples include corn oil, vegetable oil, sunflower oil, soybean oil, canola oil, cottonseed oil, and safflower oil. Processed at high temperatures, they undergo oxidation, generating free radicals. Primarily found in processed foods and baked goods, they are high in omega-6 fatty acids, which promote inflammation, leading to heart disease, arthritis, diabetes, and even cancer.

— Cereals

Cereals are made from refined grains, added sugar, GMOs, glyphosate, hydrogenated oils, artificial food colourings, and dyes, as well as additives like Butylated hydroxyanisole (BHA) and Butylated hydroxytoluene (BHT), both chemical preservatives. The former is a known carcinogen, according to the State of California. Despite being listed on the EWG's dirty dozen list of unhealthy ingredients, it is sad to note that most children are often fed these cereals, especially for breakfast, which is considered to be the most important meal of the day.

— Beverages

- **Canned, bottled, or boxed fruit juices.** They may appear healthy due to the fruit content, but they are not. It is better to eat the fruit with all its beneficial nutrients, as these juices contain too much added sugar, sweeteners, preservatives, and other additives.

- **Sodas:** These drinks contain excessive amounts of sugar and high fructose corn syrup which the body converts and stores as fat, leading to weight gain. Excess sugar also promotes inflammation, which is the cause of all chronic diseases. Children should be encouraged to drink more pure, clean water instead of becoming addicted to soda.

- **Energy drinks:** These beverages also contain sugar in addition to stimulants like caffeine and *guarana*, a fruit from South America, known for containing caffeine and the amino acid *taurine*, which acts as a stimulant to enhance physical and mental performance. They may cause heart palpitations, increased heart rate, elevated blood pressure, insomnia, dehydration, and restlessness. While they may temporarily improve brain function, energy, and alertness, the associated health risks should not be ignored.

- **Sports drinks:** Gatorade, Powerade, and Pedialyte Sport, are some of the popular Sports drinks. They contain carbohydrates and electrolytes, which help professional athletes, replace water, energy, and electrolytes during and after training. However, some of these drinks contain artificial sweeteners. Gatorade Zero, for instance, contains sucralose and acesulfame potassium. Given the known effects of sugar and artificial sweeteners on health, it's advisable to consume such beverages cautiously.

— **Sodium Chloride (Table salt)**

Table salt is not healthy for use in food preparation due to synthetic chemicals added during manufacturing. After production, natural iodine lost in the process is replaced with synthetic iodine. Additionally, table salt is bleached to achieve its pure white appearance and contains anti-caking agents like *calcium silicate* and *potassium ferrocyanide* to prevent clumping. The presence of these chemicals forces the body to use 23 times its cell water to neutralise them. This process leads to the production of uric acid, which when combined with salt, forms crystals that deposit into the bones and joints, causing conditions like gout, arthritis, and rheumatism. Table salt should, therefore, be considered a poison, and its use in food preparation should be avoided.

Sea salt, on the other hand, is simply evaporated seawater and naturally contains minerals like magnesium, calcium, sodium, and potassium. It is, therefore, better for culinary use.

Himalayan salt, sourced from the Punjab region of Pakistan, is gaining popularity. Mined in the Himalayan foothills, it is believed to be the purest salt available and has nutritional benefits backed by science. It is rich in minerals, namely, potassium, iron, and calcium. It is believed that the minerals and other elements in the Himalayan salt help with the body's natural detoxification process and help with the removal of bacteria. It also contains less sodium than table salt and does not require the body to use as much water to clear out the excess as in the case of table salt. It is naturally rich in iodine, which is artificially added to table salt. It helps the intestines to absorb nutrients and lowers blood pressure. The next time you go to the grocery store for salt, why not try the Himalayan pink?

Salt intake should be limited to less than the recommended 1,500 mg daily. Even though the American Health Association recommends 1,500 mg daily, it is better to go lower to be on the safer side. Excessive salt consumption can cause fluid retention, leading to hypertension, heart disease, stroke, and some forms of kidney disease. Most of the sodium we consume comes from processed meats, canned soups, canned vegetables, chips, and other store-bought savoury snacks. Avoiding processed foods and choosing home-cooked meals instead gives one control over salt intake.

— Condiments

Tomato ketchup, sweet relish, barbecue sauce, pancake syrup, salad dressing, mayonnaise, soy sauce, teriyaki sauce, and other pre-made sauces are the unhealthy additions to the Western diet. They are often found on dinner tables at home, in restaurants, and in fast-food joints. While they are intended to enhance taste and flavour, they contain excessive amounts of sugar, sodium, or both, refined oils, and other additives. Consuming excessive amounts of these sauces regularly could negatively impact one's health in the long run.

— Protein powders

A 2018 study conducted by the Denver-based Clean Label Project examined animal and plant-based protein powders available from retail and online stores. Alongside heavy metals, the project also tested for BPA. Results showed that out of the 134 powders tested, 28 exceeded the permitted limit of BPA, which is 3 micrograms. One product contained over 25 times the allowed limit in a single serving. The report noted that the tested products were among the top sellers. Of these, 53 were found to have elevated levels of lead, mercury, cadmium, arsenic, and BPA, including protein powders certified as 'organic' by the USDA. Plant-based protein powders were found to contain twice the amount of lead per serving compared to non-plant-based powders. Moreover, plant powders were more contaminated with other heavy metals beyond recommended health guidelines.

This poses a concern for vegetarians and vegans, as plant-based protein powders contain higher levels of heavy metals compared to non-plant-based options. It is advisable for them to seek alternative protein sources. The egg-based protein powders tested, on the other hand, did not contain any lead.

— Artificial food additives

Artificial food additives are chemicals added to foods for preservation, to enhance flavour, colour, or texture, and to add mouthfeel. They are found in baked goods, sauces, yoghurts, salad dressings, chips, cereals, beverages, and more. These include *sodium nitrite, sodium benzoate,* and *potassium sorbate,* used to prevent spoilage, tartaric acid and polysorbate, as emulsifiers to stabilise and prevent water and fat in foods from separating. In addition, there are thickening agents like *carboxymethyl cellulose,* flavour enhancers such as monosodium glutamate and *disodium guanylate, hydrocolloids,* serving as thickening and gelling agents, and finally *olestra,* a synthetic cooking oil used to enhance mouthfeel. Synthetic dyes are also used for colouring.

While the FDA ensures the safety of all food additives, they still pose potential health risks. Some additives may trigger allergic reactions, especially in children, and cause more health issues. The American Academy of Paediatrics (AAP) has confirmed that several studies suggest certain food additives could impact hormones, growth, and development in children. Also, according to the AAP, some additives may increase the risk of childhood obesity and promote hyperactivity.

Always check food labels for synthetic additives and consider limiting consumption of such foods and beverages or avoiding them altogether. If you only eat whole foods, there's no need to worry about additives!

— Brominated Vegetable Oil (BVO)

Brominated vegetable oil is a toxic chemical used as a food additive to stabilise citrus flavours in beverages. Although it has been banned as a food additive in most countries, it is still used here in the US and Latin America and can be found in drinks like Mountain

Dew, Fresca, Fanta, and Squirt, as well as certain sports drinks like Powerade, Pedialyte Sport, and some pre-mixed cocktails.

As of 2013, Pepsi announced they would remove BVO from Gatorade and all their beverages.

Bromine, one of the ingredients in BVO, is known to irritate the skin and mucous membranes. Prolonged exposure to bromine may lead to headaches, memory loss, and impaired coordination. While the FDA formerly recognized bromine safe, that decision has now been reversed, yet the FDA continues to allow BVO to be used while it claims to continue further studies on its toxicity. Avoiding soda and other sugary drinks altogether can prevent BVO ingestion.

These are just a few of the food additives found in regularly consumed processed foods. Listing all additives used in food processing exceeds the scope of this book. Carefully scrutinising labels before placing food items in the shopping cart can reduce or eliminate the consumption of foods containing such artificial additives.

Remember, the most nutritious foods are those grown and harvested without chemicals, prepared at home without additives, just as Mother Nature intended.

It's Alright To Be A Little Adventurous!

Some people are hesitant when it comes to trying new foods, while others, on the contrary, are very adventurous. When it comes to nutrition, I think it is all right to be adventurous and try some new nutrient-dense foods. So go ahead and eat fruits and vegetables in all the colours of the rainbow, but also try incorporating some foods and beverages from the list below into your diet as well.

— Seaweed

Seaweed has been used for centuries by the Japanese, Irish, Scottish, Inuit, and Chinese. It is highly nutritious and very versatile and can be added to soups, salads, stews, stir-fries, and smoothies.

- It is 10-20 times richer in minerals and vitamins than land vegetables.
- Studies have shown that people who consume diets high in seaweed have fewer nutrient deficiencies.
- Eating seaweed reduces blood cholesterol, may remove radioactive and metallic elements from the body and improves digestion.
- It may help with diabetes due to its high amount of fibre, which regulates blood sugar levels and insulin.
- Since seaweed is low in calories, the fibre could help with weight loss.
- Eating seaweed can also be beneficial to thyroid health because it is rich in iodine, manganese, potassium, phosphorus, sodium, zinc, copper, chromium, and the B vitamins. It is also rich in vitamins A, C, and E, antioxidants that fight inflammation and strengthen the immune system.
- The types of seaweed include agar, arame, dulse, hijiki, kelp, kombu, nori, and wakame, as well as the blue-green algae chlorella, spirulina, and sea moss.
- Sea moss, in particular, may contain too much iodine depending on where it grew. It is best to consume in moderation.

— Kefir

Kefir is a fermented drink that can be made with milk, coconut milk, or even water. It originated in the Caucasus, near modern-day Turkey, before reaching Russia, Europe, and then North America. The name "kefir" comes from the Turkish word *"keyif,"* which means 'good feeling.'

- Kefir is high in nutrients, containing protein, calcium, magnesium, phosphorus, B vitamins, and vitamin D.
- It also contains about 60 unique species of probiotics, which are beneficial to gut health and digestion.
- However, water and coconut milk kefir are not as nutrient-rich.
- Milk kefir grains, as well as water kefir crystals, can be obtained from Etsy, eBay, Amazon, and some health food stores. If you'd like to try making your own but can't find a starter kit, I can share some free organic milk kefir grains with you.

— Sauerkraut

Sauerkraut is one of Germany's national dishes, made from shredded cabbage using a process called *lacto-fermentation*. This involves a simple process of using shredded cabbage, sea salt, and distilled water. The shredded cabbage is submerged in salty water in a glass jar and sealed. *Lactobacillus*, a probiotic, then begins to grow in the brine, converting all sugar in the cabbage into lactic acid, resulting in that delicious vinegary taste.

- Sauerkraut is highly nutritious and healthy, making it an excellent addition to a balanced diet. It provides the body with probiotics and vitamin K2.
- It is better to eat probiotic-rich foods like sauerkraut instead of taking probiotic capsules, which may contain synthetic fillers.
- It feeds the gut with beneficial bacteria, thus improving digestion, facilitating nutrient absorption, strengthening the immune system, and reducing the risk for diseases.

- Always check ingredients and avoid sauerkraut that has been fermented in vinegar instead of brine, or pasteurised sauerkraut.

— Kimchi

This is a traditional Korean dish made with vegetables such as Napa cabbage, Korean radish, garlic, onions, ginger, and chilli peppers. It is prepared using the same process as sauerkraut, the only difference being the addition of more vegetables and spices. Some recipes even include shrimp paste added to the vegetables before fermentation.

- Kimchi is also nutrient-dense but low in calories, just like sauerkraut.
- It provides the body with vitamins A, B, C, and K, as well as iron, folate, and sodium.
- Kimchi strengthens the immune system, reduces inflammation, and may prevent yeast infections, as well as slow down the ageing process.
- It may aid weight loss as part of a calorie-controlled diet.

— Kombucha (Manchurian tea)

This is a fermented drink made with green or black tea, sugar, and a SCOBY (symbiotic culture of bacteria and yeast). Believed to have originated in Manchuria, Northeast China, its name is reported to be derived from Dr. Kombu, a Korean doctor who first brought the fermented tea to the emperor of Japan. In addition to having all the benefits of tea, it also contains probiotics that provide the gut with beneficial bacteria, which may aid in improving digestion.

Ideally, I recommend sauerkraut and kimchi, but most of my clients tell me they hate sauerkraut and kimchi and instead prefer kombucha. It is not as nutrient-dense as the fermented vegetables, but if that is what works for you, fine. Just know that it contains a lot of sugar and may not be suitable for diabetics, as there is no science yet to back its use by diabetics.

— Apple Cider Vinegar (ACV)

Apple cider vinegar is made when yeast is added to apple juice. The yeast breaks down the sugar, converting it to alcohol. Bacteria are then added, converting it into acetic acid. The yeast, bacteria, and pectin form the 'mother.' Like the probiotics mentioned above, apple cider also contains beneficial gut bacteria as well as additional benefits below:

- It speeds up digestion by activating the enzymes in the stomach and pancreas.
- It helps in absorbing minerals like calcium, magnesium, and iron.
- It also helps absorb vitamins K, C, and B12.
- It helps activate enzymes that break down protein into amino acids.
- It helps with *Small Intestine Bacterial Overgrowth* (SIBO), which is bacteria growing in the small intestines instead of the large if the pH is not high enough in the stomach.
- It improves acid reflux, which happens when stomach contents flow back into the oesophagus because there is not enough stomach acid for the valve to close. ACV helps the valve to close and improves acid reflux. Drinking a tablespoonful of ACV with 8 oz of water before a meal helps with occasional acid reflux.
- It helps release bile from the liver into the gallbladder, thus causing less bloating.
- It aids weight loss by making glucose more sensitive and by reducing insulin production.
- It helps lower cholesterol and blood pressure.
- It helps stimulate white blood cells to speed up and fight infections.

- It helps prevent bad breath. A tablespoonful of ACV in an 8-oz glass of water at bedtime prevents waking up with morning breath.

Given that disease begins in the gut, it would be a great idea to incorporate any of these gut-friendly beverages into your daily diet to decrease the risk of diseases. Instead of drinking soda or juice, how about some apple cider vinegar in a glass of sparkling water now that you know the benefits? Be sure to get organic, raw, unpasteurised ACV with the 'mother.' The smell and taste are not too bad once you get used to it. Use a straw to protect tooth enamel from the acid in ACV.

— Green tea

Green tea originated in China. It is made from tea leaves, which do not undergo the oxidation process used in black tea. Instead, they are heated using steam and then quickly dried to prevent darkening and loss of flavour. It is advertised as one of the healthiest teas on the planet due to its abundance of antioxidants.

- It is very rich in *polyphenols,* beneficial compounds found in plant foods that help reduce inflammation and even prevent cancer.
- It contains a catechin, *epigallocatechin-3-gallate,* (EGCG) a natural antioxidant that helps prevent cell damage.
- It can control the formation of free radicals by protecting cells from damage.
- It also contains traces of minerals like calcium, magnesium, phosphorus, potassium, and other trace elements beneficial to good health.
- It can boost metabolism and help burn 3 to 4% more calories, thus aiding weight loss when used as part of a calorie-controlled diet.

— Whole grains

If you enjoy rice, then you might want to consider trying whole grains such as black, purple, or red rice, instead of white.

Purple rice has its origins in Japan and is believed to be a type of grass seed. Despite its black appearance, it turns purple when cooked due to its *anthocyanin* pigment. Anthocyanin is a *flavonoid* that gives fruits and vegetables a bluish or purple colour. Blueberries, blackberries, black grapes, purple cabbage, purple potato, and eggplant are all examples of foods rich in anthocyanin.

- Purple rice may possess anti-inflammatory properties.
- Studies have linked purple rice to cancer prevention in rats.
- Being a whole grain, it is high in fibre, which may help with weight loss and help lower cholesterol and blood pressure.
- It is a good source of protein, which vegans should take advantage of.
- It is also a significant source of iron.

Red rice is grown in various regions worldwide, including India, Brazil, Sub-Saharan Africa, and Madagascar. Similar to purple rice, it contains anthocyanin, which gives it a reddish colour.

- It has anti-inflammatory properties and may lower blood pressure.
- Unlike white rice, it has a low glycaemic index, so it does not cause blood sugar spikes.
- Rich in soluble and insoluble fibre, it helps with digestion and promotes regularity.
- It may help lower bad cholesterol which helps reduce the risk of heart disease.

- It is also rich in nutrients such as calcium, iron, magnesium, and zinc, as well as vitamins B1 and B2.

These are just a few of the health benefits of purple and red rice. For those who are able to eat grains without issues and love rice, these are two varieties of rice rich in antioxidants, minerals, and other nutrients worth giving a try. While these rice varieties may not be widely known, they are so nutrient-dense, why not consider incorporating them into your diet and eventually replacing the white rice?

— Wild rice

This is a species of grass that produces grains known as wild rice, also referred to as Canada rice, Indian rice, or water oats. Typically grown in shallow waters of small lakes in Canada and the United States, it has been used by Native Americans for thousands of years. It is a very good source of vitamins and minerals and is more nutritious than regular rice.

- Low in calories and rich in dietary fibre, it helps in preventing obesity and lowering cholesterol levels.
- It may help lower blood pressure due to its low sodium content.
- It is gluten-free and higher in protein than other whole grains, which helps build muscles.
- Its richness in niacin, antioxidants, phosphorus, magnesium, zinc, and manganese may help reduce the risk of several diseases.
- Unlike most grains, which are acid-forming, wild rice is alkaline-forming, which helps to reduce inflammation.
- It helps with constipation due to its high fibre content.

Given its exceptional nutritional profile and numerous health benefits, incorporating wild rice into one's diet, particularly for those who love grains, is highly recommended.

The Power Of Eating Hygiene

How you eat is just as important as what you eat in order to get the most nutrients out of your food. Practising good eating hygiene helps to better digest your food. The following tips should help develop good eating hygiene habits.

- Always sit down to eat.
- Relax! Avoid eating when stressed, as stress prevents digestion.
- Before starting your meal, take a moment to sit down and take a few calming breaths; the body needs oxygen for proper digestion.
- Refrain from multitasking while eating. Keep distractions like phones or television away and focus solely on the food.
- Eat slowly and ensure thorough chewing until the food is liquefied. Inadequate chewing forces the gastrointestinal tract to work harder to break down food.
- Limit liquid intake during meals to prevent dilution of stomach acid, which slows down digestion. Always drink a large glass of water approximately 20 minutes before eating. This gives a sense of fullness and helps to avoid overeating.
- Stop, to savour and appreciate the food while you eat. Think about the taste, aroma, colour, and texture of the food.
- Stop eating when you are about 80 to 85% full.
- Practising these mindful eating tips will help avoid gas, bloating, belching, and indigestion. This will enable the body to absorb the much-needed nutrients from food through better digestion.

What About Dietary Supplements?

Clients tell me from time to time that dietary supplements are not necessary when one is already eating a balanced diet. That is true. However, I once probed further only to discover that the client's understanding of a balanced diet is cereal, skim milk, and banana for breakfast, then iceberg lettuce, and deli ham, on white bread plus low-fat yoghurt with fruit on the bottom for lunch. This is not quite a balanced diet, is it?

Dietary supplements come in powder, pill, capsule, or liquid form. They are either made from food or synthetic sources and provide the body with vitamins, minerals, and antioxidants.

Ideally, we should get all these nutrients from our food. However, that is not possible because the food at our disposal today has fewer nutrients than what it used to be in the 1970s.

- Many people, especially vegans, the elderly, and people with absorption difficulties, are not getting all the nutrients their bodies need.
- Conventional farming practices like the use of synthetic fertilisers and pesticides have destroyed the nutrients in the soil needed to support healthy plant life to enable the produce to provide good nourishment.
- As a result of our food being of such poor quality, many people have deficiencies with regard to key nutrients.
- In addition to the poor quality of our food, people also make poor food choices. They choose processed foods and hardly get any nutrients from their food; rather the junk foods provide too much sugar, sodium, and synthetic additives full of toxins.
- As well as the toxins in our food, environmental toxins also cause health challenges.

- The stress of day-to-day life also makes it impossible for our bodies to digest and absorb key nutrients from food.

- Finally, the use of certain medications like *Proton Pump Inhibitors* (PPIs), Prilosec, Nexium, Prevacid, and antacids for long periods causes *hypochlorhydria*, low stomach acid. Stomach acid helps break down food for easy digestion and absorption as food moves through the digestive tract.

It is necessary to take dietary supplements to correct nutritional deficiencies and to enable our bodies to fight off these toxins. It is, therefore, advisable for all adults to take supplements to ensure that the body gets sufficient nutritional support on a daily basis for optimal health. Supplements, however, should only be taken as an accompaniment. They should not replace a proper balanced diet.

Basic Daily Supplements

1. Good quality multivitamin/minerals.
2. Vitamins D3 + K2, 2000 IU.
3. Essential fatty acids supplement, for example, fish or krill oil.
4. Zinc.
5. Magnesium.
6. Probiotics, 50 billion CFUs.
7. Antioxidants: Vitamin C, Glutathione, Astaxanthin, Lycopene, Coenzyme Q10.

- Consult with your doctor before you start taking supplements if you are on any medication.
- Be sure to get good quality natural and not synthetic supplements.

- Ensure that no GMOs are included in the ingredients by looking out for the NON-GMO Project verified logo on the supplement.

- It is better to take vitamins, minerals, and fats with food as they are best absorbed on a full stomach.

- If you have difficulty swallowing pills or have impaired digestion, get chewable, sublingual, or liquid, supplements or powders and dissolve in water.

- Supplements may also contain artificial chemical ingredients.

Look out for the following ingredients in supplements and avoid them if you can:

- Titanium dioxide
- Magnesium stearate
- Stearic acid
- Silicon dioxide
- Magnesium oxide
- Calcium carbonate
- Chromium
- Cholecalciferol (synthetic vitamin D2 and D3)
- Glucose Syrup
- Dextrose
- Dl-alpha tocopherol (synthetic vitamin E)
- High Fructose Corn Syrup

When Food Causes Health Problems

Food may be medicine, but not all foods are suitable for everyone. Due to food intolerances, allergies, and sensitivities, not everyone can eat all foods. Some people are not aware of this and continue to have issues with food without even knowing that food is the actual cause of their particular health issue.

I would like to list some of the foods that are known to cause health problems just to create awareness. In order to be able to know what foods are actually causing problems, there is the need to eliminate such foods for at least 21 days and then re-introduce them into the diet one at a time. If there is no change, then the problem may not necessarily be from food. However, if the skin, joint, sinuses, or digestive issues improve, chances are that food may be the culprit, and there is a need to work with a Functional Medicine practitioner to get to the root cause of the problem.

— Gluten

This is a protein found in wheat. Most foods made from flour contain gluten; bread, cakes, biscuits, pasta, some sauces, dressings, and others all contain gluten. In addition to wheat, rye, spelt, barley, bulgur, kamut (Khorasan wheat), triticale, and other varieties of wheat all contain gluten. Gluten intolerance makes some people sick after eating any of the foods mentioned earlier. It may be gas, bloating, or other digestive issues. According to research, gluten can trigger inflammation in the intestines, which may lead to *leaky gut syndrome* (intestinal permeability), a condition whereby the gut lining may have cracks, causing food particles and other substances to enter the bloodstream. The immune system fails to recognise these foreign bodies, so the body starts to attack itself. This further causes more inflammation, leading to autoimmune diseases like Celiac disease, which is an autoimmune response to gluten. When people who have Celiac disease consume gluten, it produces severe allergic reactions, causing digestive problems. People who are sensitive to gluten but do not have Celiac disease may experience symptoms like bloating, headaches, nausea, brain fog, abdominal pain, diarrhoea, constipation, skin problems, and even depression. It is advisable to remove gluten from the diet if any of these symptoms are being experienced.

— Shellfish

This is another food that causes allergic reactions. This usually happens within a very short time after eating shellfish. It may develop at any time even if you have previously been eating shellfish without any problems. Symptoms may include hives, itching, and swelling of the face, lips, tongue, or other parts of the body. In severe cases, *anaphylaxis*, a life-threatening allergic reaction, may occur, which causes difficulty in breathing, low blood pressure, and even loss of consciousness. When this happens, medical attention should be sought without delay.

— Nightshades

These refer to foods that contain an alkaloid, *solanine*, which could be toxic in large amounts and is believed to cause inflammation and aggravate arthritis pain. They tend to accumulate calcium deposits in tendons, cartilage, ligaments, and joints, thus promoting inflammation, which causes pain. They are tomatoes, white potatoes, eggplant, bell peppers, cayenne pepper, paprika, goji berries, and tomatillos. Although the Arthritis Foundation claims that this is not true, some people still have issues with these foods. Other symptoms of nightshade allergy, sensitivity, or intolerance include heartburn, achy joints, diarrhoea, gas, bloating, and fatigue. If you suffer from arthritis or any of these symptoms and have cause to believe that eating these foods triggers your symptoms, then try eliminating them one at a time for at least 30 days. If the symptoms persist, then chances are nightshades do not trigger your symptoms. Should symptoms stop after eliminating these foods, you may have an intolerance allergy or sensitivity to nightshades and might have to consider avoiding these foods altogether.

— Eggs

Eggs are considered to be among the top eight food allergens in the United States and the second most common food allergen in babies and children. Fortunately, about 70% of kids outgrow this allergy by the time they are 16. In addition to foods, some beauty products such as shampoos and conditioners may also contain egg proteins. Some foods that do not contain any egg proteins could still become contaminated if the food was processed in the same facility where eggs were processed. Finally, some vaccines may contain egg proteins and pose serious problems if given to people who are allergic to eggs.

Other known food allergens include dairy, peanuts, tree nuts; almonds, brazil nuts, cashew nuts, hazelnuts etc., soy, and fish. If you experience any digestive issues, skin rashes, headaches, nausea, or any problems at all after a meal made from any of the above foods, try eliminating these foods and then reintroduce them one after the other in order to rule out any intolerances, allergies, or sensitivities to these foods. If the problem persists, do see a Functional Medicine practitioner to get to the root of the problem.

Chapter 2

Hydration Is Key!

"Pure water is the world's first and foremost medicine."

— Slovakian Proverb

In addition to the nutrients discussed in Chapter 1, water is also considered a macronutrient since it is needed in large quantities for survival. Water is crucial for the proper functioning of the body to promote optimal health. While humans can go for about thirty-one to forty days without food, they can only survive three to five days without drinking fresh, pure water. The average person's body is composed of about 70% water. Therefore, it is important to ensure adequate daily water intake to stay hydrated.

Why Water Is So Important

- It is essential for transporting nutrients throughout the body; without it, cells will die.

- Without adequate water consumption, the body will poison itself with its own waste. Waste products like uric acid, lactic acid, and urea are removed from the kidneys and need to be dissolved in water for elimination.

- Water is crucial for absorption, digestion, circulation, excretion, and other bodily processes.

- It plays a vital role in carrying oxygen and nutrients to cells. Water is required for breathing since the body loses about a pint of water each day through exhaling.

- Water aids in weight management as it contains zero calories, providing a feeling of fullness without adding any calories.

- Inadequate water consumption leads to excess body fat, digestive issues, constipation, obesity, and poor organ function.

- It may help prevent kidney stones by reducing acidity in urine and removing excess salts and minerals that could form stones.

- Water regulates body temperature by releasing excess heat through sweat and maintaining warmth by raising low body temperature.

- Water fights stress by calming feelings of anxiety.

- It is essential for managing bowel and bladder disorders and headaches caused by toxin build-up.

- Water lubricates the joints.

- To maintain hydration, it is important to replace water lost through bodily fluids by drinking plenty of water.

- Drink water before, during, and after workouts.

- Start your day with two cups (500 ml) of water immediately after waking up before consuming anything else. Stay hydrated by choosing water over soda throughout the day.

Types Of Drinking Water

1. **Tap water:** Tap water originates from streams, rivers, lakes, etc., and undergoes treatment at a water treatment facility before reaching our homes. In the United States, the Safe Drinking Water Act (SDWA) regulates all public water supplies. The Environmental Protection Agency (EPA) enforces strict standards to ensure that public drinking water systems are free from contaminants such as toxic

chemicals, heavy metals, herbicides, pesticides, pharmaceuticals, and carcinogens that pose health risks.

Tap water is at risk for impurities and harmful chemicals that can be toxic to the body. Contaminants like heavy metals, pesticides, and herbicides may seep into the water through the soil. Additionally, tap water may contain bacteria, viruses, and parasites. As a result, chlorine and other harmful chemicals are added to the water supply to eliminate disease-causing germs.

To safeguard against harmful toxins in our water supply, it is advisable to invest in a reliable domestic water filtration system. This ensures that every time we turn on the tap, we receive fresh, clean, pure water.

2. **Bottled water:** Bottled water, sold in plastic or glass bottles, comes from various sources, including those used for tap water. There are different types of bottled water such as:

   i.   **Artesian well water:** This type of spring water flows freely from underground wells to the land surface. The most famous Artesian wells are found in Artois, Northern France, formerly known as the Roman city of Artesium during the Middle Ages, hence the name "Artesian." Like tap water, artesian water carries the same risk of exposure to contaminants found in untreated water. It is, therefore, not healthier than regular well water, despite manufacturer claims.

   ii. **Alkaline water:** Also known as ionised water, alkaline water undergoes *electrolysis* using an ioniser. It contains alkaline minerals and has a higher pH (*potential hydrogen*) level than ordinary water. The pH of water measures the degree of acidity or alkalinity on a scale of 0-14, where levels below 7 are acidic, and levels above 7 are alkaline. Alkaline water is claimed to neutralise acidity in the bloodstream and prevent diseases like heart disease and even cancer. However, more research is needed to validate these claims. Alkaline water contains minerals like calcium, magnesium, sodium, and potassium, essential for optimal health. Brands such as Smart Water, Essentia, Core, and Bai, available in grocery, convenience, or drug stores, are all examples of alkaline water. It is believed to help the body fight inflammation by allowing the cells to remove toxins to better absorb nutrients. While drinking alkaline water does not pose health risks, there is the likelihood of *Bisphenol A* (BPA) contamination due to the plastic bottle leaching into the water. This applies to all bottled water sold in plastic bottles.

iii. **Distilled water:** Due to the declining quality of tap water, many people choose bottled water, including distilled water. Distilled water is purified through boiling and evaporation, eliminating all impurities. Drinking distilled water is safe as it lacks harmful impurities and has a pleasant taste. However, it lacks essential minerals such as magnesium and calcium, which are present in tap water but are removed during the distillation process. Prolonged consumption of distilled water could result in mineral deficiencies in the absence of a healthy, mineral-rich diet.

iv. **Sparkling water:** Sparkling water occurs naturally at sources like wells or springs, often in volcanic regions. Carbon dioxide is dissolved into the water through high temperatures, creating effervescence. Minerals like sodium, calcium, zinc, and magnesium from the surrounding rocks give it a distinctive flavour. Examples of natural sparkling water include Perrier from France, Gerolsteiner from Germany, Pellegrino from Italy, and Mountain Valley from Arkansas, USA. Sparkling water can also be artificially made by injecting carbon dioxide into water under pressure and flavouring it with fruit essences. Examples of artificially made sparkling water include La Croix, Bubly, and others found in supermarkets and convenience stores. Sparkling water is hydrating and healthy, provided it contains no added sugar, high fructose corn syrup, artificial sweeteners, or other sweeteners. However, some individuals might not tolerate it well and experience gas and bloating, especially those with intestinal tract disorders, and should avoid sparkling water. Choose sparkling water in glass bottles instead of plastic to avoid BPA contamination.

3. **Mineral water:** Mineral water originates from springs containing various natural minerals and trace elements. It may be still or sparkling, depending on the gases present in the surrounding rocks. Mineral water must be bottled at the source to maintain its purity. It can also be artificially made by adding mineral salts to distilled water and introducing oxygen and carbon dioxide to create effervescence. Besides drinking, mineral water is used in baths (spas) and is considered therapeutic. It comes from protected underground sources, which makes it pure and safe to drink. However, it may undergo treatment to remove potential toxins like arsenic. Recent testing by the Centre for Environmental Health found high levels of arsenic in some mineral water brands. This is because arsenic occurs naturally in the earth's crust and can be found in mineral and soil deposits.

4. **Reverse Osmosis (RO):** *Reverse osmosis* is a purification process that uses a *semi-permeable membrane,* (a thin barrier with holes allowing substances to pass through it) to filter out contaminants, sediments, and microorganisms from drinking water, making it pure and safe. It is believed to remove 99.9% of water contaminants, surpassing carbon filtration. Brands like Aquafina, Dasani, and Quench are purified using RO. According to the World Health Organization, water purified using this process is low in minerals and, therefore, not good for long-term consumption. However, manufacturers like Quench claim to add minerals, electrolytes, and alkalis to the treated water to make it safe for long-term

consumption. Water treated using this process can be costly, plus there is always the risk of BPA contamination from plastic water bottles.

No matter whichever type of water you choose or find suitable for your household's needs, just remember that staying hydrated is essential for optimal health and drink enough pure, fresh water daily to enable the body to function properly.

Chapter 3

Are You Regular?

"I wish that being famous helped prevent me from being constipated."

— Marvin Gaye

To thrive, the body requires a healthy digestive system capable of processing food and absorbing essential nutrients and energy from our diet.

Stool, commonly referred to as poop, is a key indicator of digestive health. Its shape, size, colour, smell, and consistency can determine digestive disorders. If the digestive system is healthy, then one should have a strong immune system, enabling the body to effectively fight off infections and other illnesses. On the other hand, if the gut is unable to process food and eliminate waste, this could lead to various gastrointestinal disorders such as indigestion, heartburn, flatulence, bloating, diarrhoea, and constipation.

Constipation is having infrequent bowel movements; less than three per week, having very hard and difficult-to-pass stools, or the incomplete evacuation of stools. It affects approximately 15 to 20% of the US population, spanning across all age groups, with a higher prevalence among the elderly, sedentary individuals, and possibly those on certain medications. Moreover, women, particularly during pregnancy, experience higher rates of constipation due to elevated progesterone levels, which slow down the contractions that move stool through the digestive tract. While constipation itself is not a disease, it may be a symptom of an underlying condition such as *irritable bowel syndrome* (IBS), an underactive thyroid gland, or colorectal cancer.

Causes Of Constipation

- **Slow *peristalsis*,** contractions when food or fluids enter the GI tract. This could be due to *hypochlorhydria*, low stomach acid, resulting in maldigestion, malabsorption, and a magnesium deficiency. Magnesium glycinate increases water in the intestines and stimulates bowel motion. It also helps relax the muscles and nerves, which play an important role in bowel motility.

- **Poor motility in the colon:** When waste takes too long to pass through the colon that could also lead to constipation.

- **Lack of physical activity:** Being inactive for a long time or not getting enough exercise daily could also lead to constipation.

- **Medication:** Certain medications could cause constipation; *calcium channel blockers* (high blood pressure medications) relax the muscles in the blood vessels in order to lower blood pressure but could also relax the muscles in the gut leading to constipation. *Narcotic* pain medications like *hydrocodone* increase the absorption of fluids, causing a lack of fluid in the intestine and leading to the hardening of stools. Finally, prescription medications for low iron, or iron supplements could also cause constipation because the absorption of iron takes time, and whatever iron is left in the gut may lead to the hardening of stools.

- **Lack of proper eating hygiene:** Eating when stressed, eating too fast, failing to chew food properly, and drinking liquids with meals could affect digestion and lead to constipation.

- **Lack of healthy dietary fats** to lubricate stool and the lack of mucus production in the colon lining.

- **Chronic stress:** When one is stressed, there is a tendency to eat the wrong foods without paying attention to one's diet. Additionally, the effects of the stress hormones on the body could lead to slow digestion and also cause constipation.

- **Poor diet:** Processed foods lacking proper nutrition; refined sugars, and lack of fibre-rich foods lead to constipation.

- **Dehydration:** When the body does not get enough water, as the stool moves through the large intestine, it absorbs the water, and if there is not enough water, it will force some extra water from the stool, which leads to constipation.

- Finally, **a change in daily routine** could also cause constipation. Being on the road at the time when one should be having a bowel movement could make it more difficult to have one. Delayed meal times, skipping a meal, or a change of diet could all lead to difficulty in having bowel movements in some individuals.

Effects Of Constipation

Occasional constipation does not develop further complications. However, chronic, long-term constipation, if left untreated, could eventually lead to the following complications.

- **Haemorrhoids:** These are swollen and inflamed veins in the rectum and anus. This usually occurs as a result of straining to pass stools, pregnancy which puts pressure on the pelvic area and the bowel, or obesity, which puts excess pressure on the veins in the anus. Eating a fibre-rich diet and self-care practices like applying an ice pack to the anal area for about 20 minutes three or four times per week could help ease the discomfort.

- **Anal Fissure:** This is a tear in the lining of the anus. It is caused by straining during a bowel movement or passing hard or large stools. It may cause anal pain, itching, and bleeding. It should usually heal on its own within four to six weeks. Otherwise, it can be treated by a medical professional. If the condition persists or in severe chronic cases then surgery may be required.

- **Rectal Prolapse:** This occurs due to part of the large intestine slipping out of the anus. It is the result of the weakening of the rectal muscles. Besides constipation, it can also be caused by giving birth or problems with the pelvis or lower gastrointestinal tract. It can cause an inability to control bowel movements, leading to stool leakage from the rectum. This condition is treatable by a medical professional and in some cases, surgery may be required.

- **Faecal Impaction:** This is when the stool is so hard it gets stuck in the rectum. It occurs when constipation has been ongoing for a long time. It causes cramps in the stomach, pain in the rectum, bowel obstruction and the leaking of stool. It is treatable by a doctor using laxatives or suppositories. In severe cases, manual evacuation may be required.

- **Bowel Incontinence:** This is the inability to control bowel movements, leading to forced soiling. Many cases are the result of constipation or diarrhoea or a weakening of the muscle controlling the opening of the anus. It affects people differently. Some individuals feel the urge to go but are not able to make it to the bathroom in time to avoid an accident. Others do not feel the need to go before soiling themselves.

Tips For The Prevention And Management Of Constipation

- Go whenever you need to and do not suppress the urge. This will prevent reabsorbing toxins back into the system and causing one to feel uncomfortable in the gut and feeling bloated.

- Drink an 8 to 16 oz (250-500 ml) glass of warm water first thing in the morning, soon after rising.

- Wake up early and make it a habit to use the bathroom before leaving the house.

- Eat breakfast as peristalsis is triggered by food.

- Practise eating hygiene; eat in a relaxed state, do not eat too fast, concentrate on chewing the food until it becomes liquid, and do not overeat.

- Avoid being in a rush which leads to being stressed. Relax!

- Increase healthy dietary fats; avocado, olive oil, coconut oil, grass-fed organic butter, etc., as these help to lubricate stools.

- Increase dietary fibre; fresh fruits and vegetables, flax seeds, chia seeds, wheat bran, and oats.

- Avoid eating junk food.

- Stay hydrated throughout the day. Drink more water, 1 to 3 litres daily, and less caffeinated and sugary drinks.

- Get regular exercise.

- Use over-the-counter laxatives with caution, as overusing these could lead to dependency and reduce bowel function.

- Instead of OTC laxatives, try dried prunes, a natural laxative, prune juice, extra virgin olive oil, bulk-forming laxatives like Metamucil or Citrucel, or herbal formulas like senna tea.

- Do not strain to pass stools, as this will only increase the risk for rectal prolapse.

- Sit in a relaxed state on the toilet, preferably with feet on a small stool and knees bent.

- See a doctor if constipated for the first time.

- Also, see a doctor when constipation lasts for three weeks or more just to make sure it is not a symptom of something more serious.

- Finally, when there is pain or cramping in the belly, blood in stool, nausea, or vomiting, a doctor should be seen at once.

Chapter 4

Get Moving!

"Walking is man's best medicine."

— Hippocrates

Just as food is medicine, so too is movement for the body and the mind. Consistent physical activity supports a healthy immune system, reduces the risk of developing chronic diseases, and promotes emotional wellness and longevity.

According to the World Health Organization (WHO), physical activity is any bodily movement produced by skeletal muscles that requires energy expenditure. This refers to all movement including recreational activities, household chores, gardening, walking, and even just running after the children or grandchildren.

The WHO recommends that all adults aged 18 to 64 engage in at least 150 to 300 minutes of moderate-intensity aerobic physical activity weekly, or at least 75 to 150 minutes of vigorous-intensity aerobic workouts weekly, or an equivalent combination of both moderate and vigorous activities throughout the week. Additionally, it also recommends moderate or high-intensity muscle-strengthening activities involving all muscle groups twice or more weekly.

The principle of "Use it or lose it" can be applied to muscles too as muscle *atrophy,* (loss of muscle), occurs when muscles are not being used, particularly in older adults.

Types Of Exercise

The five most important types of exercise for good health, disease prevention, and longevity are:

1. **Aerobic exercises:** Aerobic simply means "with oxygen." Aerobic exercises include swimming, cycling, running, and brisk walking. These activities raise the heart rate and speed up breathing, improving blood circulation, and how the body delivers and uses oxygen. Aerobic exercises help in lowering blood pressure and blood sugar levels, reducing inflammation, and raising HDL (good cholesterol) levels. Additionally, they increase blood flow to the brain and help slow down mental decline as we age.

   In addition, aerobic workouts increase *serotonin*, a chemical that relays messages between brain cells and throughout the body. This helps regulate appetite, improve sleep, and reduce anxiety in individuals dealing with depression and other mental health issues.

The WHO recommends that any cardio workout should be done for at least ten minutes at a time for maximum benefits. Moderate-intensity exercises such as brisk walking, should be done for thirty minutes daily. The long-term health benefits of aerobic exercises include reducing the risk of cardiovascular disease, preventing diabetes, stroke, and certain cancers, and reducing the risk of mortality.

Research has shown that using muscles after a meal significantly lowers blood sugar levels. This helps to prevent weight gain, diabetes, obesity, and all its complications. Instead of lounging on the couch after a meal to watch television, It will be more beneficial to make it a habit of going for a brisk walk to help digest the food and reduce blood sugar levels.

It is worth noting that aerobic fitness declines within seven to fourteen days of inactivity. Should you take a break from workouts, there is a significant decline in physical fitness. Cardiovascular endurance, lean muscle mass, and insulin sensitivity are significantly reduced during inactivity, according to a study from the Journal of Applied Physiology. Take a short break if you need to, but resume your workouts after a short while in order not to lose your physical fitness.

2. **Strength or resistance training exercises:** Strength or resistance training exercises help to increase the strength of specific muscle groups. They help to improve strength and endurance. Weights and elastic bands are used to increase intensity during such workouts. Gyms offer a variety of equipment tailored for strength training. Strength training also helps to improve joint function, muscle, tendon, ligament, and bone strength. It also increases bone density, cardiac function, and metabolism. It prevents and reverses *sarcopenia*, the loss of muscle mass in the elderly.

   It helps to burn fat and even continues to do so after workouts. It burns calories and builds muscles, which in turn shrinks fat. The *quadriceps*, thigh muscles, is the largest muscle group in the body. They extend the leg, help with movement, and require significant energy and oxygen during workouts. Consequently, any workout involving using the legs will automatically burn more calories.

   Effective leg-strengthening exercises include squats, lunges, leg curls, and calf raises.

It is very important to strengthen the core too during your fitness routine. The core comprises muscles surrounding the trunk, including the abdominals, hip flexors, obliques, diaphragm, pelvic floor, and trunk extensors. These muscles work in harmony to maintain balance and stability. A strong core is, therefore, essential for maintaining good posture, lifting objects from the ground, and rising from a chair.

The Centres for Disease Control and Prevention (CDC) recommends at least two days of strength training per week.

3. **Flexibility exercises:** Flexibility exercises are essential for overall fitness and health. They enable the body to move through its full range of motion, and are a must for every adult, particularly the elderly. Stretching increases flexibility, making day-to-day activities easier to manage. Flexibility exercises help with mobility and reduce the risk of injury. In addition, they also help with muscle recovery post-workout. Studies have shown that flexibility decreases with age, which is why most elderly people have mobility issues due to stiffness and tension.

   This is a result of the body being unable to go through its full range of motion during its younger years, so it progresses to a point where movement becomes restricted. Muscles get sore and stiff due to physical activity or repetitive movements done frequently in the course of the day. To prevent this, flexibility exercises are essential for adults, keeping muscles and joints supple and preventing injuries during physical activity. Additionally, they enhance posture, facilitating an upright stance. Flexibility exercises include yoga, Pilates, Barre, tai chi, and stretching. Ideally, these exercises should be performed for five to seven days, for five to ten minutes each session, for maximum effectiveness.

4. **Balance and coordination exercises:** Balance and coordination exercises are crucial for maintaining equilibrium during daily activities such as walking, bending, and rising up from a chair. Balance exercises strengthen the muscles

that help the body to stand upright. Examples of balance exercises include balance walks, single-leg lifts, squats, one-foot balancing, and weight shifts.

5. **Deep breathing:** Exercising makes the muscles work harder, causing the body to use more oxygen and produce more carbon dioxide. In order for the body to cope with this extra need, breathing increases from about 15 times per minute when the body is at rest to about 40-60 times per minute during exercise. It is, therefore, very important to take deep breaths while exercising. Each inhale provides the body with fresh oxygen, which fuels the muscles. The more the movement, the greater the need for oxygen to support the body to keep up with the workouts. Deep breathing also helps to relieve pain, lower blood pressure and improve digestion.

Benefits Of Exercise

Exercising regularly has many benefits as follows:

- It reduces the risk for long-term chronic diseases like type 2 diabetes, coronary heart disease, stroke, and certain cancers.
- It decreases the risk for stiff arteries, which, in turn, reduces the risk for cardiovascular diseases. (CVDs)
- It strengthens the bones, heart, and other muscles, facilitates day-to-day activities, and prevents falls.
- It lowers cholesterol and blood glucose.
- It reverses or prevents insulin resistance.
- It improves heart and lung function.
- It prevents muscle, tissue, and bone density loss.
- It suppresses cellular inflammation.

- It reduces the risk for injury, especially in older adults.

- It reduces the mortality rate by 30%, thus increasing life span.

- It increases *dopamine*, a neurotransmitter, used by the nervous system to send messages to nerve cells, which helps to improve mood and mental health, thus reducing the risk of stress, anxiety, depression, and other mental health issues.

- It improves memory and brain function, promoting mental alertness due to the increased levels of dopamine.

- It boosts *serotonin*, aka the body's "feel-good" chemical, a chemical produced by nerve cells, which improves mood by making people feel happy, as well as improve sleep, since serotonin works with melatonin to control sleep.

- It controls appetite.

- It helps with weight control by increasing metabolism.

- It slows down the ageing process. Researchers have discovered that exercise keeps DNA young and healthy. When it comes to slowing down ageing, there are no pills, injections, or cosmetic procedures that work better than exercise, yet it doesn't cost anything.

- Sweating during exercise detoxifies the body and improves skin tone.

Make Movement Part Of Your Daily Activities

- Avoid sitting down at a desk or on the couch watching television all day. Get up and walk from time to time.

- Get a pedometer app or a fitness tracker to track your steps, and aim for at least 7,500 to 10,000 steps daily. You will be surprised at the difference the daily 10,000 steps make to your health.

- Take the stairs instead of the elevator (lift).

- Park the car at a distance and walk to your destination to enable you to quickly reach your daily step goal of 10,000 or at least 7,500 steps.

- Get off the bus a stop or two before your stop and walk home.

- Family gatherings should include physical activity and not just eating, drinking, and movies. Find some fun physical activities suitable for all family members and make that part of your gatherings.

If you've never exercised before, it's advisable to consult your doctor before embarking on any exercise program, particularly if you have hypertension or other cardiovascular issues. Exercise should be fun, not a chore. Find workouts that you genuinely love and enjoy doing and make them part of your daily or weekly routine. It is important to avoid exercising at an intensity that is not comfortable for your fitness level in order to avoid pain and injury. Note that every individual has a different tolerance level for exercise, so it is better to stick to exercises that are within your comfort zone.

Avoiding Injury During Exercise

- Choose exercises within your fitness level. Do not attempt exercises that are too challenging. Listen to your body!

- Always start with a warm-up (jog in place or a brisk walk) before you start, and cool down at the end of the workout with a light jog or walk in order to bring down the heart rate, followed by stretching the various muscle groups to avoid injury and soreness.

- Learn to master the proper technique for any exercise of your choice.

- Wear proper footwear with arch support to avoid inflammation.

- Use exercise or yoga mats on slippery surfaces like hardwood floors.

- Do not push yourself to do exercises outside your comfort zone.

- Do not force yourself to exercise if you are in pain.

- Always allow your body time to recover by taking at least a day-off from exercising during the week. This allows the muscles to repair and rebuild, thus reducing the risk of injury.

- If you have a history of knee, back, neck, or shoulder injuries, be aware of the effects of certain exercises on these conditions, and do not attempt such exercises.

- When in pain due to workouts, and if the pain persists, do seek medical help.

Exercise And Weight Control

Exercise boosts the body's resting metabolism rate, aiding in weight control. It also promotes digestion and alleviates water retention and bloating. Lack of exercise, on the other hand, slows down the body's metabolic rate, making it use food less efficiently. This leads to weight gain, digestive issues, depression, and others. Regular physical activity is therefore essential for maintaining a healthy weight.

Sustaining a healthy weight is crucial for disease prevention and overall well-being. Body Mass Index (BMI) is a measurement that uses weight and height to determine a healthy weight.

BMI = Weight in pounds divided by height in inches squared, multiplied by 703. For instance, the BMI for an individual weighing 200 pounds and standing 6 feet tall would be $[200 / (72)^2]$ x 703 = 27.

- A BMI of between 18.5 and 24.9 is considered to be within a healthy weight range.

- Between 25 and 29.9 is considered to be overweight.

- Between 30 and 39.9 is obese.

- Over 40 is morbidly obese.

Other factors also come into play when determining BMI. Given that muscle is denser than fat, individuals who are very muscular due to activities such as bodybuilding, boxing, or athletics may be classified as obese despite having a normal weight. It's important to consider these factors when calculating BMI.

Visceral fat, or abdominal obesity, is the fat that accumulates around the internal vital organs. Since a large waist circumference is a risk factor for diseases such as diabetes, clogged arteries, heart disease, stroke, and cancer, it's crucial to reduce visceral fat with proper nutrition and physical activity. Unfortunately, neither drugs nor surgery can remove visceral fat besides diet and exercise. To maintain good health, women should aim for a waist circumference of 35 inches or less, and men 40 inches or less.

It is easier to pile on the pounds than it is to lose. Losing just one pound requires expending as much as 3,500 calories. However, no amount of exercise can out train a bad diet; no matter how much time is spent working out, it needs to be complemented with a proper diet and other lifestyle changes. Eating a healthy balanced diet, drinking lots of water, avoiding junk food and beverages, paying attention to portion control, together with a combination of different fun workouts, plus adequate sleep will increase metabolism and help lose weight.

- **Cardio workouts** like running, swimming, jogging and cycling for at least 30 minutes three to five times a week.
- **Strength training** with weights; since muscle burns more calories than fat, strength training exercises performed for 45 to 60 minutes three to four times a week will help build muscle, which will in turn help shrink fat and promote weight loss.
- **High-Intensity Interval Training** (HIIT): HIIT workouts force the body to use energy from fat instead of carbs and help lose fat efficiently. HIIT workouts include jumping jacks, burpees, high knees, mountain climbers, and others. Each

work out lasts for 40 seconds with a 20-second break for 25 to 30 minutes, two to three days a week.

Exercising daily is just as important as brushing your teeth. Work out three to five times a week, but make sure to get moving, breathing deeply, and stretching every day! Remember, movement is medicine for the body and mind.

Chapter 5

Are You Getting Enough Zzzz?

"Sore labour's bath, balm of hurt minds, great nature's second course,
and chief nourisher in life's feast."

— William Shakespeare (Macbeth)

In addition to proper nutrition and regular exercise, a full night of uninterrupted good quality sleep is crucial for optimal health. Sufficient sleep is vital for both our physical and mental well-being, as well as improving our quality of life. However, this is becoming more and more challenging in today's fast-paced world. Many individuals are working longer hours, while others stay up late surfing the internet, reaching out on social media, watching late-night television shows, or playing video games. The consequence of this lifestyle is sleep deprivation, which is adversely affecting our health, causing premature ageing, placing us at a higher risk for diseases, and making us prone to accidents.

Ideally, to easily fall asleep, *melatonin*, the hormone produced by the brain in response to darkness, should rise while *cortisol*, the stress hormone level, should fall at bedtime. However, late-evening activities like watching television or using electronic devices, emitting full-spectrum light can confuse the brain's perception of day and night. Furthermore, watching late news or crime shows, reading disturbing emails or reading distressing social media posts at night, can cause cortisol levels to rise, making it impossible to fall asleep. Additionally, being unable to digest a heavy meal eaten close to bedtime can make it harder to fall asleep.

After a restful night's sleep, we feel better physically and mentally, and are able to perform better the next day. This is so because while we are asleep, biological processes take place that are critical and without which we will be unable to function properly. Let's take a look at the importance of a good and restful night's sleep.

The Importance Of Good Quality Sleep

- We need to be in rhythm with nature; wake up at sunrise, and go to bed at sunset. This is part of *circadian rhythms*, from the Latin "circa diem," which means 'around a day.' Circadian rhythms occur in all living organisms and ensure that all body processes are carried out at various times during a 24-hour period. They are controlled by the brain's biological clock.

- It is during sleep that muscle repair, and tissue growth occur, as well as recovery of internal organs and protein synthesis.

- The brain slows down, gets rid of toxic waste, and is able to store new information while we sleep.

- The body releases hormones that control growth, stress, appetite, mood, metabolism, and other bodily functions while we are asleep.

- Inflammation-fighting *cytokines*, agents that are responsible for the immune system's response to inflammation, are also released by the immune system during sleep.

- During sleep, the activity of other neurotransmitters is suppressed by melatonin which helps to calm the brain.

Stages Of Sleep

While we sleep the brain goes through four stages of sleep. The first three stages are known as quiet sleep or non-rapid eye movement (NREM) sleep.

During the first stage of NREM sleep, which lasts for between five to ten minutes:

- Our brain slows down.
- The eye movements, heartbeat, and breathing also slow down.
- The body goes into a state of relaxation.

The second stage lasts for about 20 minutes, and during that time:

- The body temperature drops.
- Eye movements stop.
- The heart rate drops, and breathing becomes faster and sporadic.
- As we drift into sleep, we gradually become less and less aware of our environment.

The final stage of NREM sleep is the deep sleep stage, during which:

- The pulse is lowered, and the blood pressure drops, allowing blood vessels to rest and recover.
- The muscles become more relaxed.
- Breathing becomes slower.
- The biological processes begin. The immune system is strengthened, the body builds bones and muscles, the regrowth and repair of tissues begin, and hormones are secreted.

During the Rapid Eye Movement (REM) sleep:

- The brain becomes as active as when we are awake.

- The breathing and heart rate become faster.

- The muscles that move the body, arms, and legs are temporarily disabled by signals sent from the brainstem to prevent us from acting out our dreams.

- We start to dream.

- The eye movements become rapid.

When REM sleep is over, the body goes back to NREM stage two then the cycle starts all over again.

The Benefits Of A Good Night's Sleep

- Getting enough sleep strengthens the immune system and enables it to defend the body from colds, flu, and other infections.

- Adequate sleep helps prevent weight gain. Sleep deprivation triggers increased levels of *ghrelin*, the hormone that boosts appetite, and decreases the production of *leptin*, the hormone that tells the body that it is full. This contributes to overeating, leading to obesity with all its complications.

- A restful night's sleep also strengthens the heart and decreases the risk of heart disease. Lack of sleep causes the release of *cortisol*, a stress hormone. High levels of *cortisol* cause the heart to work harder, raising blood pressure, blood sugar, triglycerides, and blood cholesterol, which are all risk factors for heart disease.

- A good night's sleep promotes a better mood. Having a good night's sleep reduces anxiety, irritability, and mental exhaustion, which in turn improves mood.

- Having a good night's sleep helps to improve memory, focus, and clarity.

Effects Of Sleep Deprivation

- Sleep deprivation makes it impossible for the immune system to function optimally, which results in an increased risk for chronic diseases such as heart disease, diabetes, stroke, and infections.

- Sleep deprivation causes the accumulation of toxic waste products in the brain, and increases the risk for cognitive decline and dementia.

- The central nervous system does not function optimally due to lack of sleep, which disrupts how the body sends and processes new information.

- Lack of sleep increases the risk of injury. Physical and mental exhaustion due to sleep deprivation causes accidents on the road and even at home.

- Lack of sleep also negatively affects our mental and emotional state of mind. One may struggle with anxiety, irritability, anger, sadness, and even suicidal thoughts.

How Much Sleep Is Required For Optimal Health?

The amount of quality sleep needed for optimal health and well-being varies according to age. Below is a table showing the number of hours of sleep recommended for each age group.

Age Group	Hours of Sleep
18 years and above	7 - 9
11 – 17 years	8.5 – 9.5
5 – 10 years	10 - 11
3 – 5 years	11 - 13
1 – 3 years	12 - 14
3 – 11 months	14 - 15
0 – 2 months	12 - 18

Preparing For A Restful Night's Sleep

- Make it a habit to go to bed and wake up at the same time and stick to that schedule.

- Do not go to bed on an empty or full stomach. Allow at least 3 hours between dinner and bedtime. However the meal should not be too heavy to enable the digestive organs to rest instead of being busy digesting food.

- Turn off the television, computer, phone, and other electronic devices about an hour before bedtime.

- Limit liquid consumption before bedtime to avoid having to go to the bathroom too many times during sleep.

- Ensure that the bedroom is dark, cool, and quiet. Invest in dark and heavy curtains or blinds to keep the bedroom free from light, as well as a fan to keep the room cool.

- Get regular exercise during the day as it promotes better sleep at night.

- Limit caffeine consumption during the day as its stimulating effect can interfere with a good night's sleep.

- Self-care practices like taking a warm bath, deep breathing, and relaxation techniques, as well as gentle stretching at bedtime, can relieve stress, anxiety, and fatigue, promote relaxation, and help you fall asleep faster. Also, diffusing some essential oils like lavender, or drinking herbal teas like chamomile, lavender, lemon balm, valerian, or passion flower, promote relaxation and help to fall asleep and stay asleep.

Avoid Sleeping Pills

Some individuals struggle to fall asleep and may resort to sleep medication or over-the-counter sleeping pills. However, these tend to be habit-forming and should only be for short-term use. The more these pills are taken, the more the body gets accustomed to them, potentially causing dependency, which could lead to addiction over time. Instead of relying on sleeping pills, try exercise, deep breathing, and other self-care practices to induce sleep naturally. If you must take a sleep aid, try a melatonin supplement for a short time only. If it doesn't help, discontinue use.

Given that sleep deprivation is also a factor as far as our health struggles are concerned, in addition to nourishing our bodies, staying hydrated, and being physically active, a full night of uninterrupted good quality sleep is also crucial for our health and well-being.

Some individuals claim they only need just four hours of sleep to be able to function the next day. This practice can lead to sleep deficit, which is the difference between the amount of sleep the body needs and how much it actually gets. This causes mental and physical exhaustion making it impossible to function properly. Moreover, it increases the risk for accidents, infections, and chronic diseases.

Don't let anything stop you from getting a good and restful night's sleep.

Sweet dreams!

Chapter 6

Beware Of High Stress Levels!

"Adopting the right attitude can convert a negative stress into a positive one."

— Hans Selye

Stress, if not properly managed, can contribute to long-term health struggles. In addition to proper nutrition, hydration, physical activity, and sufficient sleep, stress management is therefore also essential for optimal health.

I often hear clients expressing feelings of being under a lot of stress. So, what exactly is stress? It's a state of worry or nervousness characterised by mental, physical, or emotional strain. Stress is a normal human reaction, the body's response to challenges that may arise from thoughts or situations bringing about feelings of anger or frustration. It is commonly experienced when we find ourselves in situations beyond our control. Examples of such situations include:

- Financial obligations that cannot be met.
- Loss of income or the loss of assets.
- Office stress; a domineering boss, having to work long hours, working under dangerous conditions, discrimination or harassment at the workplace,
- Injury or long-term illness.
- Emotional issues like anxiety, depression, low self-esteem, guilt feelings, and fear of the unknown, especially what is reported by the media.
- Having to deal with a disaster, a pandemic, or any other traumatic event individually or collectively

- Major life changes like moving, marriage, adoption, divorce, and the loss of a loved one.

All of the above situations are stressors that can adversely affect one's health if not properly managed.

Types Of Stress

There are 3 main types of stress as follows:

- **Acute stress:** This is short-term stress, stress that lasts for a short time, from minutes to hours. It is stress that is experienced when stuck in traffic, after an argument, or when one is criticised. This kind of stress is good because it motivates one to work on one's personal growth. It helps develop patience, self-esteem, and self-control.
- **Episodic stress:** When acute stress is experienced too often, it becomes episodic. For instance, experiencing frequent, uncontrolled anger, frequent acid reflux or other gastrointestinal issues, anxiety or panic attacks, and being stuck in traffic for long hours daily.
- **Chronic stress:** When the challenges, frustrations, or threats that cause stressful situations are experienced consistently for long periods, the result is chronic stress.

The Fight-Or-Flight Response

This is the body's automatic, healthy reaction to a frightening or stressful situation.

Whenever the body senses a threat or danger, the sympathetic nervous system is activated, triggering a stress response preparing the body to fight or flee. This response is designed to enable the body to survive in threatening or dangerous situations. There are three stages of the fight-or-flight response, namely, alarm, resistance, and exhaustion.

— Alarm stage

This initial stage causes the central nervous system to be awakened, causing the body to gather its defences. This is characterised by:

- An increased heart rate
- Increased blood pressure
- Rapid breathing
- Dilation of pupils
- Release of the stress hormone cortisol by the adrenal gland.
- Increased energy due to an increase in *adrenaline,* a hormone that helps the body's response to stressful situations.

— Resistance stage

During this stage, the body begins to repair itself after the initial shock of a stressful event or situation as follows:

- A lower amount of cortisol is released
- The heart rate goes back to normal

- The blood pressure also goes back to normal
- Despite all these recovery efforts, the body still remains on high alert

— Exhaustion stage

When the body constantly goes through stressful events or situations, it finally goes into the exhaustion stage, leading to chronic stress. At this stage, the body has used up all its resources by trying to recover from the alarm stage but failing to do so. As a result, the body begins to experience distressing symptoms as follows:

- Increased resting heart rate
- High blood pressure
- A rise in blood sugar
- Increased perspiration
- Dilated pupils
- Heartburn or indigestion
- Weight gain
- Stomach ulcers
- Insomnia
- Increased risk for type 2 diabetes
- Increased risk for infections
- Decreased immune function
- Depression

Long-Term Effects Of Chronic Stress On Health

Stress is not always a bad thing because it is a healthy, natural, physical response that helps to increase our awareness in difficult situations. However, when it becomes chronic, it puts one's health at risk and leads to long-term, life-threatening health challenges. The long-term effects of chronic stress are:

- Premature ageing
- Chronic fatigue syndrome
- Increased risk for a heart attack
- Heart disease
- Stroke
- Irritable bowel syndrome (IBS)
- Alzheimer's disease
- Tension headaches
- Insomnia
- Muscle pain
- Mental health issues
- Obesity
- Increased accumulation of toxins in the body by negatively affecting the enzymes responsible for detoxification.

Managing Chronic Stress

There is no cure for chronic stress; doctors may only prescribe medications to ease the symptoms. However, it can be managed through lifestyle changes.

Eating a healthy diet by eliminating processed foods and refined sugars can help reduce the negative effects of stress on the body and even assist in managing chronic diseases such as high blood pressure and high blood sugar, which may be caused by stress. Additionally, staying well-hydrated by drinking plenty of fresh, pure water can help flush out stress-related toxins.

Another essential lifestyle change for stress management is regular physical activity. Being physically active daily is good medicine for both the body and mind in the fight against stress. Exercise can lower stress levels while simultaneously improving fitness and overall health. It lowers levels of cortisol and adrenaline, the body's stress hormones. Lastly, it promotes the release of *endorphins*, chemicals in the brain that help uplift mood and alleviate pain.

Practising self-care activities like the following will help maintain physical, emotional, and mental well-being, and also help with managing chronic stress.

- Taking a hot bubble bath.
- Getting a massage.
- Getting a manicure and pedicure.
- Going for a walk.
- Practising mindfulness and meditation.
- Listening to some relaxing music.
- Practising deep or diaphragmatic breathing.
- Getting regular and adequate sleep.
- Reducing the intake of caffeine and alcohol.

Aromatherapy can be a natural remedy for stress relief. Essential oils trigger a powerful, calming, and relaxing effect on the body and mind. They also support the nervous system and help with balancing emotions, thus impacting the hormones and adrenal glands. The oils can be diffused in a room, added to a bath, used for a massage, or diluted with carrier oils like sweet almond or coconut oil and applied to pulse points.

- Lavender, chamomile, and rose essential oils promote deep relaxation and relieve stress.
- Valerian and chamomile oils induce sleep.
- Bergamot, Clementine, and grapefruit oils help with depression.
- Lemon, citronella, and sweet orange oils alleviate anxiety.

Spirituality also forms an integral part of the holistic approach to alleviating stress. It requires belief in a higher, Supreme Being and the release of negative emotions such as anger, bitterness, resentment, regret, and grudges. Additionally, it involves focusing on positive emotions like love, peace, joy, compassion, and hope. Resolving conflicts through forgiveness and seeking forgiveness, then living in harmony. Prayer and meditation on the holy book bring one closer to God, which fosters inner peace and improves mental health.

Hobbies are also another great way to reduce stress. They help focus on the activity of the moment and take the mind off work or whatever the stressor is. They enable one to unwind after a busy working week, thus reducing stress. Music, one of my favourite hobbies, has a calming effect on the mind. Whether it's listening to music, playing a musical instrument, or dancing to music, all these activities help reduce stress. A hobby is to help unwind. It is, therefore, important to choose activities that do just that and avoid anything that will add more stress, like complicated and challenging puzzles and word games. Also, hobbies should be in no way related to, or remind you of work. They should be completely different from what one does for work. Activities like gardening, reading, drawing, and painting are excellent for unwinding and reducing stress. Any fun or creative activity that one enjoys should help take the mind off stressors.

Furthermore, it is important to mention that herbs also help to reduce stress. *Ashwagandha*, an *adaptogen*, herb or natural substance that helps the body adapt to stress, is an Ayurvedic herb used in Indian traditional medicine for centuries to relieve stress and anxiety, increase energy levels, and improve concentration and mental focus. Other adaptogens such as *Lion's mane, Maitake*, and *Reishi* are mushrooms that promote calmness, reduce anxiety and stress, improve sleep, and boost memory. *Schizandra* is another adaptogenic herb that balances hormones and helps deal with stress. It has been used in Traditional Chinese Medicine (TCM) for thousands of years to improve the body's resistance to stress, toxins, and anxiety.

Finally, pets can play a significant role in stress management. According to research, the stress hormone cortisol and blood pressure could be lowered simply by petting a dog. In addition, the heart rate slows down, breathing becomes regular, and tension in muscles is relaxed. Interacting with animals has a calming effect on the mind, reducing loneliness and boosting mood. Having a pet and bonding with it provides companionship and is beneficial for mental health. Pets also protect children from anxiety, according to the CDC. The great impact of pets on mental health should not be underestimated.

In dealing with chronic stress, it is therefore advisable to consider getting a 'furry friend.'

Chapter 7

Toxins Are Everywhere!

"In our world, these endless lists of toxic chemicals consistently assault our immune system."

— David Wolfe

In order to achieve optimal health, constant exposure to *toxins* (poisonous substances), which weakens the immune system, causing health problems, should be avoided.

- Toxins prevent the supply of oxygen to the body.
- They prevent the production of haemoglobin.
- They lower protection against oxidative stress.
- They increase the risk for chronic diseases like cancer, diabetes, heart disease, and stroke.
- They accelerate the ageing process.

Unfortunately, these toxins are everywhere; in the air, our water, food, and in the environment. Although we are not able to totally eliminate these toxins, knowing their source and avoiding exposure as much as possible will help us reduce the *toxic load*, the accumulation of harmful chemicals in the body over time.

There are three main ways that toxins can get inside the body.

1. Through direct contact, touching the skin, dermal absorption, and eyes, via personal care products and cosmetics that we use daily, and through household cleaning products.

2. Through the inhalation of gases, vapours or mists, and dust via the nose, air passages, and lungs.

3. Through the digestive system by means of the foods and beverages that we ingest.

The toxins that enter the digestive system are filtered by the liver and converted into waste products, which are eliminated by the body. However, toxins that enter through the lungs and the skin can go straight into the bloodstream and are later carried by the blood to the rest of the body. We have to be careful what products we slather on our skin or are exposed to through inhalation. We could be unknowingly exposing ourselves to harmful toxins.

Toxins That Pollute Indoor Air

Pollutants in the environment can be man-made (chemical) or occur naturally (biological). These include *endocrine disruptors*, chemicals that mimic our natural hormones, and carcinogens. They are emitted as gases in the home from various products made with synthetic chemicals, posing a health risk by polluting indoor air.

Chemical pollutants include *volatile organic compounds* (VOCs), which consist of a wide range of chemicals such as benzene, toluene, formaldehyde, ethanol, methanol, and others. According to the Environmental Protection Agency, VOC levels can be two to five times higher in indoor air than they are in outdoor air due to their presence in numerous household products. Common sources of such toxic chemicals in the home include:

- **Mattresses** that are coated with flame-retardant chemicals during manufacturing and emit small amounts of formaldehyde.
- **Carpets/rugs** treated with stain guard chemicals, benzene, styrene, and other carcinogenic substances.
- **Wooden furniture/flooring** that releases formaldehyde and polyurethane used as a liquid finish.
- **Upholstered furniture** coated with flame-retardants and stain guard chemicals.
- **Wall paint** contains toluene, benzene, ethanol, formaldehyde, and lead.
- **Personal care products and cosmetics;** such as toothpaste, mouthwash, shampoo, body wash, antiperspirant deodorant, body lotion, and other skincare and hair care products, contain numerous chemical ingredients. According to the FDA, the average household uses at least nine personal-care products daily containing a whopping 126 chemical ingredients including; parabens, sulphates, alcohols, formaldehyde, aluminium, propylene glycol, fragrances, phthalates, benzophenone, and styrene, all which cause allergic reactions in some individuals. The Environmental Working Group also confirms that there are twelve toxic chemicals and contaminants in cosmetics such as; formaldehyde (a known carcinogen), paraformaldehyde, methylene glycol, quaternium-15, mercury, dibutyl, isobutyl, and isopropyl (parabens), polyfluoroalkyl (PFAS) carcinogens, M-and O-phenylenediamines (used in hair dyes), which may damage DNA and cause cancer. Hopefully, with this information, cosmetics and personal care products containing all these toxic, difficult-to-pronounce ingredients will be replaced with those containing natural and environmentally friendly ingredients as much as possible.

- **Make-up,** including foundation, powders, mascara, lipstick, concealer, blusher, and nail polish, all contain toxic chemical ingredients such as lead, asbestos, phthalates, formaldehyde, and others, which can cause hormonal imbalance, infertility, and cancer.

- **Prescription drugs** contain hydrochloric acid, benzyl chloride, acetone, toluene, and other organic compounds

- **Household cleaners and disinfectants.** Harmful chemicals such as ammonia, bleach, triclosan, chlorine, ethylene glycol, and others are harmful chemicals found in everyday household cleaners. These chemicals emit toxic fumes and can cause irritation to the skin, eyes, nose, and throat. In addition, they may cause asthma and breathing problems, eczema, and other skin conditions, particularly in children.

- **Laundry detergents and dryer sheets** contain formaldehyde, phthalates, chlorine, benzene, sodium laureth sulphate, and other harmful chemicals, including 1,4-dioxane, one of the most hazardous chemicals found in laundry soap. Due to its toxicity, Tide laundry detergent was banned in Europe because of its high levels of dioxane, which is present in greater amounts in Tide compared to other laundry soaps. These harmful chemicals may be absorbed through the skin from fabrics washed in detergents and have been linked to cancer. A 2022 study found dioxane in all laundry detergents, including even plant-based ones. Dryer sheets contain the most harmful chemicals found in household cleaners, laundry detergents, and fabric softeners. They all contain fragrances; that include dozens of harmful chemicals and allergens. These chemicals cling to fabrics and may require ten to fifteen wash cycles to completely remove any chemical residue from fabrics. These harmful chemicals gradually penetrate the body through the skin and lungs, affecting the endocrine and nervous systems and causing allergic reactions such as hives, eczema, and other skin rashes. Finally, when dryer sheets are exposed to heat in the dryer, they release volatile organic compounds (VOCs) through the vent into the environment.

- **Dry-cleaned clothing:** The most common chemical used for dry cleaning is perchloroethylene, a solvent harmful to the nervous system and a carcinogen. It also pollutes the environment. Perchloroethylene residue remains on garments long after cleaning, and with each subsequent cleaning, the residue increases, exposing the wearer to higher levels of the chemical. With regard to employees at the dry cleaners, constant exposure to this chemical raises their risk for cancer of the kidneys, liver cancer, and depression.

- **Ozone from appliances:** Appliances such as printers, copiers, televisions, and computers emit ozone. Although considered an outdoor pollutant, ozone pollution is now very common indoors. Ozone pollution in homes can damage the lungs, especially in combination with other pollutants. Researchers from West Virginia University discovered that an individual's genetic and metabolic profile could be altered by microscopic nanoparticles from laser printers through inhalation. Just by using a laser printer, one is unknowingly inhaling small nanoparticles to the detriment of one's health. Additionally, unintentionally inhaling the printer/photocopier black carbon may cause eye irritation and headaches. Accidentally touching it may cause skin irritations, posing health risks.

- **Electromagnetic field (EMF):** EMF, also known as radiation, is produced by the flow of electricity through electrical devices like computers, cell phones, wireless devices, Bluetooth devices, televisions, electric blankets, microwave ovens, Wi-Fi routers, and other electrical appliances. EMF is believed to cause biochemical and physiological changes, including oxidative stress, allergic and inflammatory responses, additionally affecting the tissue repair process, which increases the risk for cancer.

- **Room fresheners:** The use of room air fresheners contributes to indoor air pollution due to volatile organic compounds (VOCs) such as ethyl benzene, toluene, and formaldehyde released into the air. These VOCs may cause eye, nose, and throat irritation, nausea, and headaches.

- **Insecticides and pesticides:** Chemicals used to control insects, ants, cockroaches, flies, mosquitoes, rodents, weeds, and mould in homes often contain diazinon, which affects the nervous system, acephate which can stimulate the nervous system causing dizziness, nausea, respiratory problems, and even death. Finally, carbaryl can cause headaches, nausea, vomiting, blurred vision, abdominal pain, and also affect the nervous system and kidneys.

- **Toilet deodorisers:** Toilet bowl deodorisers and cleaners contain harmful chemicals like hydrochloric acid, isopropyl alcohol, phenol, and others, which could lead to impaired lung function, nausea, headaches, and even damage to the nervous system.

- **Tobacco products:** Second-hand smoke can pollute indoor air, posing respiratory health risks.

Biological Indoor Pollutants

Biological pollutants are not easy to see because they travel mostly through the air. The most common indoor pollutants include mould, bacteria, viruses, dust mites, animal dander, and pollen.

- **Mould:** Thrives in environments with increased moisture and poor ventilation. Exposure to mould causes wheezing, sinus problems, itchy eyes, headaches, and ear infections. Prolonged exposure can lead to digestive disorders, mental illness, and even cot death in infants.

- **Bacteria and viruses:** Typically found in dirty areas, particularly in the kitchen. There are four types of bacteria common in the home namely, *Staphylococcus aureus, Micrococcus, Pseudomonas,* and *Bacillus.* They can be found on surfaces, in food, and in water. Staphylococcus aureus can be found in the air, water, and soil. It can also be found in the human nose and on the skin. Staphylococcus is a group of bacteria responsible for most food-borne diseases worldwide. This is due to improper food handling practices. It also causes nasal infections. Micrococcus is found in dust, water, and meat products. It is reported to be the cause of pneumonia, meningitis, septic arthritis, and endocarditis. Pseudomonas, on the other hand, thrives in moist areas in the home, such as drains, baths, and sinks. It can cause a number of infections like pneumonia, septicaemia, blood, and urinary tract infections. The last of the common bacteria found in the home is the bacillus. This can also be found in dust, water, soil, fruits and vegetables, and raw and even processed foods that are not properly refrigerated, if not served immediately. There are three species of this bacterium, some of which cause spoilage in food as well as food poisoning. Others cause infections, while other species are not harmful to humans.

- **Dust mites:** These are tiny insect-like pests that occur naturally and thrive in warm, humid, and dusty areas of the home. They are so small they cannot be seen with the naked eye. They lurk on fabrics, mattresses, beddings, carpets, and upholstered furniture and feed on dead human skin cells. Dust mites trigger allergy symptoms such as sneezing, runny nose, itchy and watery eyes, and asthma symptoms.

- **Animal dander:** Furry pets in the home like dogs, cats, rabbits, and hamsters, normally shed dead skin. These dead skin cells are known as dander. Pet dander can trigger allergic reactions, such as rashes, hives, and asthmatic symptoms upon direct contact.

- **Pollen:** Pollen from seed-bearing plants travels indoors through open doors and windows and causes sneezing, runny nose, and itchy and watery eyes in people who have *allergic rhinitis,* also known as hay fever.

- **Radon:** This is an odourless and invisible radioactive gas naturally released from the breakdown of uranium in soil, rock, and water. It is commonly found in basements. However, even homes without basements may still have elevated levels. Nearly one in fifteen homes in the US has more than the acceptable levels of radon. Prolonged exposure to radon could cause lung cancer.

Major Outdoor Air Pollutants

The World Health Organization estimates that more than 90% of the world's population breathes unsafe air. As we step outside our homes, we are exposed to invisible gases that we inhale unconsciously. These include:

- **Volatile Organic Compounds (VOCs):** Released into the atmosphere from painting, dry cleaners, nail salons, auto body workshops, and petroleum fuels. Regular exposure to high levels of these vapours can lead to headaches, difficulty breathing, asthma attacks, eye, nose, and throat irritation, bronchitis, respiratory problems, and even premature death.

- **Carbon monoxide:** A toxic gas that is both invisible and odourless. Generated by vehicles on the road and machinery burning fossil fuels. Indoor sources include gas or kerosene space heaters and gas or oil furnaces. Inhaling high levels of carbon monoxide reduces the amount of fresh oxygen needed by the heart and brain, potentially leading to unconsciousness and even death. It may also trigger angina in individuals with heart disease.

- **Methane:** A colourless, odourless, and hazardous greenhouse gas, mainly produced by livestock (cows, sheep, goats) through manure decomposition and belching. It affects climate change due to its contribution to increased warming in the environment. Other sources include landfills, underground coal mines, fossil fuel production, wastewater treatment, combustion engines, and other industrial processes. Like carbon monoxide, excessive inhalation of methane can decrease oxygen intake, resulting in headaches, blurred vision, nausea, and memory loss.

- **Ozone:** Composed of three oxygen atoms, ozone is a colourless, odourless, gas found in the earth's upper atmosphere and also at the ground level. The upper ozone is formed naturally and protects from the harmful ultraviolet rays of the sun. However, at ground level, it becomes a harmful air pollutant affecting people and the environment. Inhaling ozone can reduce lung function, leading to lung infections, shortness of breath, coughing, chest pain, throat irritation, asthma, and bronchitis.

Reducing Exposure To Toxins

In our modern world, it is almost impossible to totally eliminate the sources of pollution. However, we can try to minimise exposure to indoor pollutants by taking the following steps:

- **Use of Air Purifiers:** Portable air purifiers can help reduce indoor air pollution, although they may not completely eliminate pollutants from the air.

- **Limit EMF Exposure:** Turn off cell phones and other smart devices at bedtime, or switch them to airplane mode if possible, to reduce electromagnetic field (EMF) emissions. While EMF protection necklaces are available, their effectiveness is uncertain. It's advisable to limit exposure to EMF by reducing the use of such devices.

- **Ventilation:** Keep windows open daily and use fans to increase airflow indoors. According to the EPA, the use of dehumidifiers can reduce moisture, particularly during colder months when windows cannot be left open, helping to prevent mould growth.

- **Cleaning:** Regularly vacuum mattresses and pillows to control dust mites. If you have pets, vacuum pet beds, carpets, rugs, curtains, and couches regularly, wash pillowcases, couch covers, and curtains to remove dust mites and pet dander.

- **Houseplants:** Houseplants help purify indoor air. They turn the carbon dioxide we exhale, through a process called *photosynthesis*, into fresh oxygen at night. They also remove toxic air pollutants, including benzene, formaldehyde, xylene, and toluene. Finally, they fight airborne allergies, particularly the snake plant. Others, like the spider plant, palms, and ferns, help rid the air of radon. A NASA experiment, which was published in 1989, confirmed that houseplants can rid the air of the above cancer-causing VOCs. Research also revealed that the microorganisms in the soil of household plants also help filter the air.

- **Limit Natural Gas Appliance Use:** Minimise the use of natural gas appliances indoors, as they emit nitrogen dioxide, carbon monoxide, and formaldehyde into the air.

- **Avoid Smoking Indoors:** Smoking indoors exposes individuals to second-hand smoke, which can lead to lung cancer, heart disease, stroke, and other illnesses, particularly in vulnerable populations such as the elderly and individuals who are *immunocompromised*, have a weak immune system, which affects the ability to fight infections.

- **Kitchen Ventilation:** Ensure kitchens are well-ventilated, especially during cooking times. Use exhaust hoods to limit emissions of nitrogen dioxide, carbon monoxide, and formaldehyde from natural gas cooking stoves.

- **Install Detectors:** Install a carbon monoxide alarm in the home to warn occupants of dangerous levels of carbon monoxide in indoor air, a smoke detector to sound the alarm for a potential fire, and a radon mitigation system to reduce concentrations of radon in the air indoors.

- **Use Safe Cleaning Products:** Whenever possible, use chemical-free, biodegradable laundry detergents and cleaning products that are safe for humans, pets, and the environment. When using toxic household cleaning products, wear Personal Protective Equipment (PPE) such as masks and gloves to avoid inhaling fumes or direct skin contact.

- **Clean, non-toxic, Skincare:** The skin swallows everything it comes into contact with, which is later absorbed into the bloodstream. It is, therefore, advisable to avoid slathering products containing toxic ingredients that we wouldn't ingest on the skin.

- **Handling Cash Register Receipts:** Cash register receipts are coated in BPA-absorbing toxins that can penetrate the skin so deep that they cannot be washed off. Avoid carrying them around, as studies suggest that individuals who handle large numbers of such receipts may have higher levels of BPA in their bodies.

- **Room Fresheners:** Avoid aerosol spray room fresheners and instead use essential oils for room freshening when needed.

- **Personal Hygiene Products and Cosmetics:** Consider natural alternatives to highly toxic personal hygiene products and cosmetics. Skincare and haircare products for women of colour, in particular, tend to be more toxic. Studies have revealed that women of colour have higher levels of beauty product-related toxins in their systems. Women of colour should avoid the use of chemical hair dyes, hair relaxers and straighteners, skin lighteners, deodorants, and feminine hygiene products containing toxic oestrogenic ingredients such as parabens and phthalates, which have been linked to hormone-sensitive cancers such as breast, ovarian, uterine, endometrial cancers, uterine fibroids, and infertility.

- **Nail Care Products:** Minimise exposure to nail varnish and nail varnish removers, as well as nail polish dryers. A recent study published in Nature Communications revealed that frequent use of ultraviolet nail polish dryers could damage DNA, thus causing cell death in the hands. The study goes on to say that frequent exposure to UV radiation emitted by nail polish dryers can also increase the risk for skin cancer.

- **Makeup Containing Talc:** Avoid makeup containing talc; pressed powder, setting powder, blush, and eyeshadow, as they may contain traces of asbestos, a known carcinogen linked to mesothelioma and ovarian cancer. A 2020 study found that 14% of make-up containing talc tested positive for asbestos. This is because talc and asbestos are minerals found close together. As a result, when talc is mined, it may contain traces of asbestos, which is linked to *mesothelioma*, a cancer found in the lining surrounding the lungs, stomach, and heart, as well as ovarian cancer. Recently, Johnson & Johnson, a leading manufacturer of personal hygiene, pharmaceutical products, and medical devices, proposed $8.9 billion to settle a talc-related lawsuit to thousands of women who claimed the J&J talcum powder was the cause of their ovarian cancer and mesothelioma diagnosis.

- **Cookware and Food Storage:** Choose cookware, bakeware, and food storage containers wisely, taking into consideration the dangers of toxic cookware discussed in Chapter 1 of this book. Do not cook with aluminium foil or saran wrap, or use any of these or plastic containers for food storage. Parchment paper is safer to use for baking instead of foil. Reduce the use of plastics. Food should not be microwaved in plastic containers, covered with saran wrap, or stored in plastic containers. Use glass or ceramics for food storage. Do not leave plastic containers with beverages, especially drinking water, in the car during the summer months. Dispose of plastic water containers that become heated. Plastic water bottles should not be refilled. Avoid freezing water in plastic bottles. Substitute paper sandwich bags for saran wrap (cling film) or zip-lock bags.

- **Food Choices:** Avoid foods that contain pesticides, herbicides, fungicides, hormones, and other contaminants. Choose organic or locally grown produce if possible. Peel inorganic fruits and vegetables. Buy hormone-free meats and other products to avoid ingesting hormones and pesticides. Buy only wild-caught fish and seafood. Eat home-cooked meals instead of boxed dinners, and always read labels and be on the lookout for synthetic ingredients.

- **Air Pollution:** Plant air pollution-absorbing trees such as Norway maple, Ginkgo Biloba, Oak, Black Walnut, and Yew, known for absorbing carbon emissions.

- **Water Filtration:** Invest in a reliable water filter for drinking water and a carbon shower head filter, to remove chlorine and heavy metals to prevent dry, itchy skin and other skin problems.

- **Fragrances:** Use fragrances naturally made with essential oils, and opt for chemical-free, fragrance-free, skincare, hair care products and even toothpaste..

- **Healthy Lifestyle Habits:** Maintain a healthy lifestyle by drinking plenty of pure, fresh water, exercising daily, practising deep breathing, getting adequate sleep, minimising alcohol consumption, reducing intake of sugar, salt, and processed foods, taking dietary supplements to avoid nutritional deficiencies, managing stress, and occasionally fasting to rid the body of toxins.

Foods That Help Flush Toxins Out Of The Body

Foods rich in antioxidants help the body rid itself of toxins. Below is a list of antioxidant-rich foods and spices that help the body with detoxification. You most probably already have some, if not all of these items in your kitchen, and incorporating them into your daily diet will give the body what it needs to flush out toxins.

- **Almonds:** Rich in antioxidants, particularly vitamin E and selenium, almonds help neutralise harmful free radicals, support enzymes that aid detoxification, and help the liver with the production of *glutathione*, the body's master antioxidant, which controls inflammatory processes and facilitates the excretion of toxins from the body.

- **Beetroot:** High in *betalains*, a phytonutrient responsible for its red colour, betalains are known to have anti-inflammatory, antioxidant, anti-cancer, and detoxification properties, helping to boost the body's detoxification process.

- **Blueberries:** Packed with antioxidants, flavonoids, and vitamin C, including the antioxidant *anthocyanin*, which provides the bluish colour and helps fight oxidative stress. They increase blood flow to the kidneys to enable them to filter out toxins effectively.

- **Broccoli:** Rich in *glucosinolates*, compounds found in cruciferous plants. Glucosinolates are converted in the body to *isothiocyanates*, which are known to boost detoxification by enhancing the liver's ability to neutralise cancer-causing substances.

- **Chia Seeds:** High in fibre, chia seeds promote regularity, aiding in toxin elimination from the body.

- **Garlic:** A natural antibiotic and antioxidant, garlic contains *allicin*, which helps the liver produce enzymes that filter toxins from the digestive tract. Its sulphur content helps produce *glutathione*, which neutralises oxidative chemicals and eliminates them from the body as well as slows down the progression of cancerous cells.

- **Ginger:** With antioxidant and anti-inflammatory properties, *gingerol* in ginger helps reduce oxidative stress and stimulates digestion and bowel movement, which helps to cleanse accumulated waste and toxins from the colon and other organs.

- **Green Tea:** Green tea is loaded with nutrients and polyphenols that fight free radicals in the body and prevent oxidative stress that leads to the accumulation of toxins. *Epigallocatechin gallate* (EGCG), a type of catechin found in green tea, boosts the production of enzymes that help with detoxification in the liver, helps protect it from toxins, and lowers the risk of certain cancers.

- **Kale:** A nutrient-dense, cruciferous vegetable, kale is rich in antioxidants like vitamin C, *beta-carotene*, *quercetin*, and *kaempferol*, antioxidants that help fight oxidative stress and damage caused by free radicals, thus supporting the body's detoxification process.

- **Lemons:** Rich in vitamin C, an antioxidant that helps protect the body from free radicals, lemons neutralise free radicals, aid digestion, and break down toxins in the liver for elimination through the kidneys.

- **Seafood:** Varieties like algae, crayfish, krill, salmon, shrimp, and trout contain *astaxanthin*, a powerful antioxidant, that fights inflammation, reduces oxidative stress, detoxifies the harmful effects of free radicals, and boosts the immune system.

- **Turmeric:** Containing *curcumin*, a powerful antioxidant, turmeric combats free radicals and boosts levels of glutathione, which detoxifies harmful toxins in the body, converting them into compounds that can easily be eliminated. Lastly, it promotes bile production in the liver to eliminate fat-soluble toxins from the body.

- **Watermelon:** With 92% water content, watermelon promotes hydration, which is crucial for effective processing and elimination of toxins. It is also rich in lycopene, an antioxidant that neutralises harmful free radicals in the body and helps protect from cell damage.

Chapter 8

Herbs & Spices That Heal

"Herbs are the friend of the physician and the pride of cooks."

— Charlemagne

Herbs and spices are the parts of a plant; leaves, seeds, roots, and bark, which are used in cooking, flavouring, and food preservation.

Herbs refer to the leafy green or flowering parts of plants, which can be used either fresh or dried. Spices on the other hand, are derived from the seeds, bark, roots, and fruits of plants and are generally used dried.

Both herbs and spices have many uses including cooking, food preservation, medicinal uses, and religious rituals. They could also be used topically on rashes and other skin conditions, as well as for problems on the hair and scalp.

Interestingly, some pharmaceutical drugs are derived from herbs. For instance, morphine comes from the poppy plant, aspirin from willow bark, and digoxin from foxglove.

Herbs originated in temperate climates such as England, France, and Italy. Most spices, on the other hand, come from warm tropical regions such as India, which produces about 75% of the spices used worldwide, the Caribbean 'Spice Island' Grenada, Sri Lanka, and the Arabian Peninsula.

Both herbs and spices have powerful health benefits. Using them to cook will not only enhance the flavour of dishes but will also improve our health due to their medicinal properties.

Why Incorporate Herbs And Spices In The Diet

- Herbs and spices have antioxidant properties due to the chemical compounds they contain.

- They are anti-inflammatory.

- They are *anti-tumorigenic*, preventing the formation of tumours.

- They are anti-carcinogenic, prevent the effects of carcinogens, or stop the development of cancer.

- They have blood pressure, cholesterol, and glucose-lowering properties.

- They protect against cardiovascular disease.

- They protect against *neurodegeneration*, the gradual loss of the functioning of cells that receive and send messages to the brain.

- They have *immunological* properties and immunity to toxins or infections.

- It is better to supplement our diet naturally with herbs and spices, than to take supplements containing synthetic ingredients, or even drugs.

- They add flavour, colour, and aroma to food.

- They can be used to reduce salt intake; basil, black pepper, coriander, dill, and ginger can be used in cooking to replace salt.

Most Commonly Used Herbs And Spices

— Allspice

i. Allspice berries are the fruit of a tropical tree in the myrtle family from the West Indies. It is a unique spice with the flavour of four different spices; cinnamon, nutmeg, pepper, and cloves.

ii. The berries contain the compound *eugenol*, which makes them rich in antioxidants.

iii. Allspice is used mostly in West Indian and Caribbean cooking especially for the famous Jamaican Jerk seasoning for chicken.

iv. In North America and Europe, it is used mostly in cakes, cookies, and other baked goods.

v. In the food industry, it is used for pickles, ketchup, canned fish, and some preserved meats. It is also used for flavouring mulled wine.

vi. It may help to reduce inflammation, nausea, stomach upsets, and other intestinal problems. It can also help maintain healthy blood pressure levels.

vii. In traditional medicine, it is used for toothache, rheumatism, and other common ailments.

— Anise/Aniseed

i. Anise is one of the oldest known spices. Native to the Middle East, it is now grown in North Africa, Spain, Mexico, and other temperate regions.

ii. It contains the compound *anethole* and is rich in many nutrients. It has antifungal, anti-bacterial, and anti-inflammatory properties.

iii. It is sweet and aromatic with a typical liquorice flavour.

iv. It is used in fish, seafood, and poultry dishes as well as in breads, cakes, cookies, and other baked goods. It is also widely used in making candies.

v.   It is the base for many liquorice-flavoured liqueurs and aperitifs; Ricard, Pastis, Ouzo, and Sambuca.

vi.   It may help with indigestion, constipation, stomach cramps, and flatulence. It may also help with stomach ulcers and maintain normal blood sugar levels. It is used to treat bronchial disorders in Ayurvedic medicine.

vii. People with any condition that could be made worse by being exposed to oestrogen; endometriosis, breast, ovarian and uterine cancers should avoid using anise.

— Basil

i.   Basil is considered a sacred herb native to India. It is also grown in Africa and Iran.

ii.   The herb contains the compound *eugenol*, which has anti-inflammatory, antibacterial, antifungal, and antioxidant properties.

iii. There are different species; holy basil, purple, Thai, and lemon, but the most popular is sweet basil.

iv.   It is widely used in Mediterranean cooking, especially in Italian cuisine.

v.   It is a natural *calcium channel blocker* (lowers blood pressure). It also helps to boost digestion and can be used for stomach spasms, intestinal gas, and even worms. It detoxifies the body.

vi.   It should be used fresh in order to benefit from its health benefits, which are lost during the drying process.

vii. Basil should be used with caution, especially by people taking blood pressure medications, as too much of it may cause low blood pressure. Also, since it contains vitamin K, which helps blood to clot, ingesting too much of it may interfere with blood thinners such as *Warfarin*, and *Coumarin*, which are prescribed to prevent the formation of blood clots.

— Bay leaf

i. Also known as bay laurel, sweet laurel, or sweet bay, it is native to the humid climate of the Mediterranean region.

ii. It contains *eugenol, flavonoids, alkaloids,* and *phenol.*

iii. Unlike most herbs, bay leaves are used dried instead of fresh. The leaves are usually added whole but removed before the dish is served.

iv. They are used mostly in Mediterranean cuisine and added to other Mediterranean herbs like rosemary oregano and thyme. In French cuisine, it is the essential part of a *bouquet garni* with the addition of parsley and thyme.

v. Bay leaf tea is believed to have anti-inflammatory, antibacterial, and even anti-cancer properties. According to the Journal of Nutrition Research, the compounds in bay leaf help protect the body from the effects of cancer-causing free radicals.

vi. It is believed to lower blood sugar levels, improve digestion, treat respiratory ailments, fight against infection, and even stop hair loss, promoting healthy hair growth. It also lowers cholesterol levels and protects heart health.

vii. Ingesting too much bay leaf may cause drowsiness and sleepiness.

— Black pepper

i.   Black pepper comes from black peppercorn, which is the fruit of the *piper nigrum* plant. It is native to India but is grown in other tropical countries; including Vietnam, Sri Lanka, and Brazil.

ii. It contains the alkaloid *piperine,* which makes it pungent. It is known as the 'king of spices' because it has such a strong aroma.

iii. It is used to season and spice fish and meats as well as vegetables, soups, salad dressings, and others.

iv. Piperine helps reduce oxidative stress. It also lowers the risk of cardiovascular disease, lowers blood pressure and bad cholesterol, and increases good cholesterol.

v.   It is high in antioxidants and may reduce damage caused by free radicals. It fights inflammation and helps to improve insulin sensitivity.

vi. It may slow down the reproduction of cancer cells.

vii. People who suffer from allergies and asthma should be careful not to inhale black pepper as it may trigger sneezing and coughing. Also, ingesting too much black pepper may cause stomach upsets and bleeding in people with bleeding disorders.

— Cardamom

i.   This spice is grown in southern India, Sri Lanka, Tanzania, Vietnam, and Guatemala. It is one of the most expensive spices in the world and is known as the 'queen of spices' in India.

ii. It contains *cineole,* a very powerful antiseptic, and is high in antioxidants.

iii. It is usually paired with sweet spices such as cinnamon, nutmeg, allspice, and cloves.

iv. Its distinctive flavour makes it suitable for use in a wide variety of dishes; sweet and savoury, in stews, curries, and rice dishes, as well as cakes, cookies, and pastries.

v. It is also used to flavour beverages like coffee and chai tea.

vi. It may lower blood pressure and help with weight loss. It may also help with digestive disorders such as indigestion, heartburn, constipation, irritable bowel syndrome, and intestinal gas, as well as colds, coughs, and bronchitis.

vii. Some individuals may experience allergic reactions to this spice, such as skin rashes, difficulty in breathing, diarrhoea, and abdominal pain.

— Cayenne pepper

i. This spice is believed to have originated from Cayenne in French Guiana. It is now grown in the United States, Mexico, India, and East Africa.

ii. It contains the compound *capsaicin*, which produces heat and is responsible for the burning sensation.

iii. It could be used fresh or as a dried powder. It may also be a blend of a variety of chilli peppers.

iv. It is used in all hot sauces as well as stews and casseroles, fish, and meat dishes. It is also used in egg dishes.

v. Capsaicin acts as a *vasodilator*, preventing muscles in the walls of arteries and veins from tightening to enable blood to flow easily through the vessels. This helps to keep blood pressure levels within normal range. It increases the production of nitric acid and reduces inflammation.

vi. It boosts metabolism, improves digestion, and relieves pain. It may be applied to joints to relieve pain.

vii. Ingesting too much of this spice may cause heartburn or an upset stomach. It may also interfere with blood thinners.

— Cilantro & Coriander

i.   These are different parts of the same herb. Cilantro refers to the leaves of the herb. Coriander, on the other hand, is the dried, ground seeds used as a spice in traditional Indian cooking. This herb originated in Southern Europe and the Middle East but is now grown in many other parts of the world.

ii. Cilantro contains the natural chemical compound *aldehyde*, as well as *cineole*, a powerful antiseptic.

iii. It is widely used in European, Asian, Caribbean, and Latin American cuisines. It is best to use cilantro fresh and at the end of cooking in order to preserve its distinctive flavour. It is a very good source of vitamins A, C, and K.

iv. It has anti-inflammatory and anti-microbial properties.

v.   It may help prevent heartburn and other digestive issues. It may also help reduce swelling in the joints.

vi. Coriander acts as a diuretic. It may lower blood pressure as a result of removing extra sodium from the body. It also lowers bad cholesterol and reduces the risk for coronary heart disease. It may also lower blood sugar.

vii. Cilantro may cause itching or hives in some individuals when it comes into direct contact with the skin. Secondly, the *phytoestrogens*, (oestrogen-like compounds found in plants) in coriander, may cause contractions in the uterus. As a result, expectant and nursing mothers should avoid using cilantro and coriander.

— Cinnamon

i.   Real cinnamon, also known as Ceylon cinnamon, comes from Sri Lanka. It is the bark of a tropical tree. It is also grown in Seychelles and other tropical countries. The cinnamon found in grocery stores is not real cinnamon but rather cassia, which is mostly grown in China. Unlike cassia, cinnamon bark is thinner and more brittle and has a more delicate fragrance. Also, true cinnamon is a tan brown, while cassia, on the other hand, is of a darker brown colour.

ii. It contains the organic compounds *cinnamaldehyde, cinnamate,* and *cinnamic* acid.

iii. Cassia, on the other hand, contains a naturally occurring compound, *coumarin*, but true cinnamon only contains traces. Ingesting excessive amounts of coumarin (more than six grams daily) can cause liver disease.

iv. Cinnamon is widely used worldwide in both sweet and savoury dishes. It is used in cakes, biscuits, pastries, and other baked goods. It is also used to flavour curries and other sauces in Asian cooking.

v. The cinnamaldehyde in real cinnamon has anti-inflammatory properties and can reduce the inflammatory response in chronic diseases like diabetes, high blood pressure, heart disease, and arthritis, thus reducing the symptoms of these conditions.

vi. Real cinnamon also contains vitamins, minerals, and antioxidants. It is rich in beta-carotene, which promotes healthy eyesight. Drinking cinnamon tea with honey will ease stomach cramps, indigestion, diarrhoea, and other stomach problems.

vii. Real cinnamon is generally safe, but some individuals may experience allergic reactions like irritation and soreness in the mouth and lips if consumed in excess. The coumarin in cassia, on the other hand, may interfere with *acetaminophen*, pain and fever medication, *statins*, (high cholesterol) medications, and other medications that affect the liver, thus increasing the risk for liver damage.

— Cloves

i. Cloves are native to the Spice Islands in Eastern Indonesia (the Moluccas), but they are also grown in Madagascar, Sri Lanka, Tanzania, and Grenada.

ii. The spice contains the compound *eugenol*, which acts as a natural anaesthetic.

iii. Cloves are used in Middle Eastern, Indian, and North African cooking to flavour curries, sauces, and rice dishes. In Europe and North America, they are used in baking.

iv. Cloves are high in antioxidants, vitamins, and minerals. They help to fight free radicals and reduce the risk of developing heart disease, diabetes, and even cancer.

v. Chewing cloves or drinking cloves tea after dinner improves digestion and helps relieve acidity, constipation, flatulence, and diarrhoea. Cloves also stimulate hair growth due to the presence of vitamin K, which promotes better blood circulation to hair follicles. It is also good for the treatment of dandruff and itchy scalp. The antioxidants in cloves may prevent or delay greying of the hair.

vi. In Ayurvedic medicine, cloves are used for circulation, digestion, and metabolism. They are also used to promote good oral hygiene, ease toothache and gingivitis, and promote fresh breath.

vii. Consuming too much cloves may cause damage to the kidneys and liver.

— Dill

i. Dill is native to the Mediterranean region, Asia Minor, and South Eastern Europe but is now cultivated in India, North America, and Europe.

ii. The major compounds in dill are *limonene* and *phellandrene,* as well as *phenolic* acids, which give it antioxidant, antimicrobial, and anti-tumour properties.

iii.   The herb is used in salads, sauces, or on fish. The seeds, on the other hand, are used as a spice. They can be crushed or used whole in soups, pickles, vegetable dishes, bread, and salad dressings.

iv.   Dill is used in Scandinavian, Russian, and other Eastern European dishes.

v.   Dill seeds are used to treat digestive problems, flatulence, nausea, and loss of appetite. They may also treat urinary tract infections and painful urination.

vi.   In Ayurvedic medicine, dill tea is a traditional remedy used to treat respiratory and digestive problems. The seeds are also chewed as a breath freshener.

vii.   Consuming dill in excessive amounts may cause diarrhoea, vomiting, and allergic reactions like swelling of the tongue, throat, and skin rashes.

— Fennel

i.   Fennel is native to the Mediterranean, but it is cultivated in many other countries including India, China, France, Germany, and others.

ii.   It contains the compound *anethole* and is rich in antioxidants, *beta-carotene*, which the body converts to vitamin A, plus vitamin C, which is necessary for collagen production and protects against cellular damage, as well as flavonoids like *quercetin*. It has anti-inflammatory, antibacterial, and anti-cancer properties.

iii.   All the parts of this herb, the fronds, stalk, bulb, and seeds, are edible. It has a mild, sweet, aniseed flavour. It can be used fresh in salads and slaws. The seeds pair well with fish and seafood dishes. It is also used to flavour liqueur.

iv.   Anethole acts as an appetite suppressant, and drinking fennel tea before a meal makes one less hungry and, consequently, consuming fewer calories.

v.   Fennel is used in Ayurveda to treat asthma and bronchial disorders. The seeds are used for tea, which is believed to be a digestive.

vi.   Fennel should be avoided by people with conditions such as breast, ovarian, uterine, cancers, and endometriosis as it may mimic oestrogen.

— Garlic

i.   Garlic is actually considered to be a vegetable and belongs to the onion family, but it falls within the definition of a herb which is a plant with leaves, seeds, or flowers used in flavouring food or has medicinal properties.

ii.   It is believed to have first been cultivated in the Mediterranean region or in the Caucasus, the region between South Eastern Europe and the Black Sea, and was brought to North America by the European settlers and to Europe by the Roman Invaders. Today, it is grown all over Asia, North Africa, and North and South America, mostly in temperate regions.

iii.   It is used in salad dressings, sauces, vegetable and meat dishes, soups, and stews. It is also used to make garlic butter. It can be eaten raw since the more garlic is cooked, the less potent it becomes.

iv.   It contains the compound *allicin* and is also loaded with antioxidants. Allicin has antibacterial properties and helps fight infections. It may also help lower blood pressure, cholesterol, and blood sugar, as well as prevent certain cancers.

v.   It boosts the immune system and helps fight coughs, colds, and flu.

vi.   It may prevent Alzheimer's disease and dementia.

vii.   Garlic is a natural blood thinner and should not be consumed by people on blood thinners as this may increase the risk of internal bleeding.

— Ginger

i. It is believed to have originated in India, China, or both. It is not certain where it actually came from. It is now cultivated in Nepal, Central America, Africa, the Caribbean, and certain states of the US.

ii. It contains the compound *gingerol*, which makes it pungent, gives it anti-inflammatory properties, and reduces oxidative stress.

iii. It may be beneficial for anxiety, depression, dementia, and Alzheimer's disease.

iv. It helps with digestion, nausea, and other gastrointestinal discomfort.

v. Gingerol may help with cancer prevention by inhibiting the growth of cancer cells.

vi. It may aid weight loss by reducing inflammation in the gut and making the body more insulin-sensitive.

vii. People taking blood-thinning medications, pregnant and lactating women should not consume ginger.

— Mint

i. There are several varieties of mint but spearmint is the one most often used for culinary purposes. It is believed to have originated from Europe and Asia but is now grown in North America and Africa. It got its name from its spear-shaped leaves.

ii. It contains the compounds *limonene* and *carvone*. It also contains antioxidants, vitamins, and other vital nutrients.

iii. Besides being used in cooking, it is also used to flavour candy, chewing gum, toothpaste, and mouthwash. It can also be used in making tea.

iv. Carvone helps to inhibit digestive muscle contractions, and this helps to ease symptoms of digestive upsets, abdominal pain, constipation, diarrhoea, and irritable bowel syndrome.

v. It helps to protect against, and repair damage caused by free radicals, and may help to improve memory as well.

vi. It helps women with hormonal imbalances.

vii. Consuming too much may lead to androgen imbalance and may also cause liver damage.

— Nutmeg

i. Nutmeg is the seed of a tropical tree that is native to the Spice Islands in Indonesia. Today, Grenada is one of the largest producers. It is also grown in Sri Lanka, Malaysia, and the West Indies.

ii. It contains *myristicin,* a compound that occurs naturally and is found in some herbs and spices.

iii. It is used in Southeastern Asian dishes, baked goods, desserts, and beverages like mulled cider and mulled wine. It is used in Ayurvedic medicine to promote sleep. It can also be used to spice tea and coffee.

iv. It is a good source of vitamins and minerals.

v. It is a very rich source of antioxidants and may help with heart disease, sugar spikes, and cancer, plus it protects against premature ageing.

vi. It acts as an antidepressant, improves mood, and promotes a good night's sleep.

vii. Consuming too much, more than 5 grams at a time, may lead to toxicity and could even be fatal.

— Oregano

i. Oregano is native to the Mediterranean region and Southwestern Eurasia. It belongs to the mint family. Its name comes from Greek, which means 'joy of the mountains.'

ii. It contains flavonoids, *thymol,* and other compounds.

iii. It is also rich in antioxidants, vitamins A, C, and K, as well as iron, magnesium, potassium, and other minerals.

iv. It has antimicrobial, antiviral, and antifungal properties.

v. It may have anti-cancer properties. One test-tube study experimented on human colon cancer cells with extracts of oregano, which is believed to have killed the cancer cells.

vi. Oregano can be used fresh, dried or as an oil.

vii. Individuals who are allergic to mint should avoid oregano as it could cause an allergic reaction in such people.

— Parsley

i. Parsley originated in Southern Europe and the Eastern Mediterranean but is now grown in so many regions. There are two main types, curly and flat-leaf, but there are many subspecies as well.

ii. It contains antioxidants, carotenoids, flavonoids, folate, vitamins A, C, and K, and other nutrients, as well as phenolic compounds. It is very nutrient-dense yet very low in calories.

iii. It has antibacterial, antifungal, diuretic, *analgesic, immunosuppressant,* (prevents the immune system from mistakenly attacking healthy cells), anti-diabetic, and other properties.

iv. It supports bone health due to vitamin K, which increases bone mineral density. As a result, it reduces the risk of fractures. The carotenoids in parsley, *lutein beta carotene,* and *zeaxanthin,* as well as vitamin A, are all nutrients that protect the eyes and may prevent macular degeneration, a major cause of blindness.

v. It may improve heart health due to its richness in folate.

vi. It works as a diuretic and helps reduce blood pressure. It reduces joint pain and swelling. *Apigenin,* an antioxidant in parsley, helps reduce inflammation and prevents cellular damage.

vii. Parsley should be avoided by pregnant and lactating mums as well as people on medications like Warfarin. Individuals with kidney disease should avoid consuming parsley in excessive amounts

— Rosemary

i. Rosemary is native to the Mediterranean region, North Africa, and Asia Minor, and belongs to the mint family.

ii. It is a rich source of antioxidants and anti-inflammatory compounds.

iii. It pairs well with poultry and is used in a variety of dishes like stews, soups, casseroles, and salads.

iv. Rosemary tea can reduce various types of inflammation, thus relieving pain and swelling. It stimulates hair growth and is said to be as powerful as *Minoxidil,* the leading prescription drug for hair loss, especially in the case of *alopecia areata,* an autoimmune disease.

v. Inhaling rosemary essential oil relieves anxiety and lowers cortisol, the stress hormone. It also improves memory and concentration and fights damage to the brain by free radicals.

vi.   Studies suggest that extracts of rosemary may inhibit tumour growth and stop cancer cells from multiplying.

vii. Rosemary should be avoided by pregnant and lactating women as higher doses may cause a miscarriage in the case of the former.

— Sage

i.   Sage also belongs to the mint family and is also native to the Mediterranean and coastal regions of Southern Europe. The best sage, however, is said to come from Dalmatia in Croatia.

ii.   The major compounds in sage are *cineole* and *camphor*. It is also high in antioxidants, vitamins A, C, E, K, and minerals like zinc, copper and magnesium.

iii. In cooking, it is used in sausages, winter squash recipes, stuffing, cured meats, and pasta dishes.

iv.   It helps lower blood sugar and cholesterol levels and acts as an expectorant, getting rid of mucus from the respiratory tract.

v.   It alleviates symptoms associated with menopause, stimulates the release of the hormone *oestradiol*, and promotes ovarian function.

vi.   It helps to ease digestive problems, heartburn, indigestion, gas, bloating, and diarrhoea. Burning sage is believed to improve mood, memory, and focus, as well as get rid of negative energy.

vii. Avoid using sage before, during, and after surgery as it may interfere with blood glucose control.

— Thyme

i. Thyme is native to the Mediterranean region and extends from Southern Europe to North Africa. It is one of the oldest herbs and was used in ancient Egypt to embalm the Pharaohs.

ii. There are different varieties of thyme, but many of these are not for culinary use. The most common ones used in cooking are the common or garden thyme and lemon thyme. It is used mostly in savoury dishes; fish, meat, and vegetables, as well as in marinades, soups, and stocks. It can also be used to make tea.

iii. Thyme is made up of flavonoids and *salicylic acid,* as well as vitamins A, C, and magnesium.

iv. Thyme is believed to have antiseptic and antispasmodic properties. It is also anti-inflammatory, antiviral, and antifungal.

v. It is believed to protect the brain from premature ageing by increasing omega-3 fatty acids. It may also prevent memory loss.

vi. It boosts immunity, lowers blood sugar and cholesterol levels, and relaxes blood vessels that constrict and restrict blood flow.

vii. Consult your doctor before taking thyme tea if you are on medication, as it could interfere with certain medications.

— Turmeric

i. Turmeric is a member of the ginger family. It comes from the underground rhizomes of the plant. Even though it is native to India, it is also grown in Indonesia, South America, and the Caribbean.

ii. *Curcumin* is the active compound in turmeric and is known for its powerful anti-inflammatory effects.

iii. Turmeric is used to colour foods, mainly curry powder, mustards, butter, and rice dishes. It is also used in soups, smoothies, and teas.

iv. It protects against heavy metal toxicity by binding up heavy metals in order to expel them from the body. It also improves bile flow to enable the removal of toxins from the body.

v. It improves heart health and prevents Alzheimer's and cancer. It eases arthritis joint pain. Drinking golden milk made with turmeric and warm coconut milk is believed to relieve joint pain.

vi. Curcumin acts as an antidepressant by promoting *neurogenesis,* the formation, and development of new nervous tissue needed for mood control.

vii. Turmeric acts as a natural blood thinner and should be avoided by people on blood thinning medications. Also, consuming too much turmeric may cause low blood sugar.

These are just some of the health benefits of herbs and spices. Lately, more and more people are becoming aware of the powerful effects of these herbs on health and are now turning to homemade remedies for common ailments using these herbs and spices.

Chapter 9

Fasting Also Heals!

"Fasting is the greatest remedy, the physician within."

— Paracelsus, father of toxicology

Yoshinori Ohsumi, a Japanese cell biologist and professor at the Tokyo Institute of Technology's Institute of Innovative Research, was awarded the 2016 Nobel Prize in Physiology or Medicine for his discovery of *autophagy*.

Autophagy originates from two Greek words: "auto," meaning self, and "phagy," meaning eating. Autophagy, or self-eating, is the natural process of cellular recycling within the body. Through this process, old and damaged components within a cell are broken down and reused to build new cells. This process is essential because damaged components can overcrowd the cell and prevent it from functioning properly. Autophagy, therefore, targets cellular thrash for removal. It also causes the destruction of bacteria and viruses and decreases inflammation, thus holding the key to the reversal of diseases. This process, however, can only be maximised through **fasting**.

Types Of Fasting

Fasting is the practice of abstaining from food and drink for a specified period. For cellular rejuvenation, fasting is recommended for at least 24 to 48 hours. Below are various types of fasts for cellular benefits:

- **Dry fasting or absolute fast:** With this fast, there is no eating or drinking water or liquids throughout the fasting period. This fast is not suitable for beginners or people who are not used to fasting. The duration of this fast depends solely on the individual and how long they can go without water. This type of fast could lead to dehydration and should, therefore, not be practised for long periods at a time.

- **Water fast:** This fast restricts eating but allows drinking unlimited amounts of water for a period of 24 to 72 hours or more.

- **Liquid fast:** This fast restricts eating solids, requires no chewing at all but, allows drinking water, homemade fruit juices, bone broth, and soup.

- **The veggie juice cleanse:** Also known as juice fasting. This fast allows drinking only vegetable and fruit juice throughout the fasting period, usually 1 to 3 days.

- **Intermittent fasting:** This is a time-restricted eating whereby one fasts for 14, 16, 18, or 20 hours and only eats during a particular time frame.

- **Alternate day fasting:** This is the practice of alternating the days of fasting and eating. It could be 24 hours of fasting, then 24 hours of eating, depending upon the individual.

- **5:2 fasting:** This is a form of intermittent fasting where one fasts for 2 days and then eats normally for 5 days.

- **Prolonged fasting:** This is fasting for up to 72 hours or more, usually under supervision in a therapeutic fasting facility, probably before a medical procedure.

- **The Daniel fast:** This fast was named after Daniel in the Bible, who only ate fruits and vegetables without any bread or meat and only drank water for 21 days. During this fast, only fruits, vegetables, whole grains, nuts, and legumes are allowed. Water is the only beverage allowed on this fast. There is no drinking tea, coffee, or juice, and no dairy, meat, eggs, or bread allowed.

What Happens To The Body When We Fast?

After fasting for only one day, *insulin sensitivity* improves. Insulin is the hormone that regulates blood sugar. Due to the consumption of refined and processed foods, most people are *insulin resistant*, a condition whereby the body does not effectively regulate blood sugar. This can lead to type 2 diabetes, heart disease, obesity, and other chronic diseases. During fasting, insulin is shut down, and the metabolic rate goes up, enabling the body to start burning stored fat.

The body then starts releasing increasing levels of the *human growth hormone* (HGH). This hormone is usually injected by athletes and people who want to grow more muscle and look younger. It is believed to be very expensive and comes with side effects, yet increased levels of this hormone can be achieved by up to about 2000% for men and 1300% for women just by fasting for 24 to 48 hours.

After fasting for about 18 hours, when the body becomes nutrient deficient, the level of mTOR (mammalian target of rapamycin), an enzyme controlled by a gene, the master controller of protein synthesis in the body drops. When the level of this enzyme drops, **autophagy** is activated. This process is critical for cells to dispose of all cellular garbage, as well as cancer cells. The healing power of each cell is turned on as a result.

Most body tissues replace their cells with new ones regularly. When autophagy is turned on, the body is in dire need of energy, so it consumes worn-out and damaged tissues, bacteria, viruses, and all other junk and recycles those to send to the bloodstream to be used for energy. Amino acids are also created from decomposed particles of previously stored protein and used to build muscle.

mTOR is the opposite of autophagy and is necessary for stimulating muscle cell growth. The absence of mTOR, or not having enough, will lead to wasting muscles (*sarcopenia*), yet when mTOR is turned on, autophagy is turned off. However, too much mTOR will lead to cancers, premature ageing, and other diseases. It is, therefore, necessary for there to be a balance between mTOR, which is a time to build (*anabolic*), and autophagy, which is clean-up time (*catabolic*).

The bone marrow starts to make new stem cells, which makes fasting the fastest way to increase stem cells for a younger, better-looking, and youthful body. Studies have shown that a 7-day water fast reduces cancer risk by 70%, as cancer cells are all likely to die during the fast.

Other Factors That Trigger Autophagy

- In addition to fasting, exercise can also trigger autophagy. High-Intensity Interval Training (HIIT) resistance training, running, jogging, and brisk long walks on an empty stomach can trigger autophagy. These workouts require a lot of energy and will force the body into autophagy in order to burn stored body fat.
- Consuming a low-carb, high-fat diet will also trigger autophagy because the body is burning fat instead of glucose for energy.
- A good night's sleep also promotes autophagy since the body is in a fasted state during sleep; that is when the cells repair and recover.

The Benefits Of Fasting

- It causes the body to switch from using glucose for energy to burning the body's fat reserves for energy.
- Insulin levels go down, but lower insulin levels signal the liver to release *glycogen*, stored blood sugar, to ensure the availability of energy.

- Oxidative stress is reduced due to an increase in the body's antioxidants. Consumption of the Western diet, as well as the process of digestion, promotes oxidative stress. Fasting is, therefore, necessary in order to reduce oxidative stress.

- It activates the healing power of every cell in the body. As a result of the body switching from burning glucose for energy to burning fat during a fast, the stem cells are triggered and become more active, leading to cellular repair and tissue regeneration.

- Metabolic disorders such as type 2 diabetes are reversed.

- Fasting eases symptoms of pulmonary disorders such as *Chronic Obstructive Pulmonary Disease* (COPD), slows down the progression of the disease, and prevents further damage to the lungs.

- It helps ease symptoms of cardiovascular disease, helps with normal cardiac development, removes plaque from arteries, and prevents *atherosclerosis*, the thickening of the arteries due to plaque build-up, in the lining of the artery.

- It heals the gut and improves digestive health. Symptoms of leaky gut, bloating, indigestion, heartburn, and irritable bowel syndrome are all reversed.

- It controls bacterial and viral infections by destroying bacteria and viruses.

- Liver cells do a better job of converting fat-soluble toxins to water-soluble for excretion.

- Immune cells in tissues surrounding the brain are rejuvenated, causing all toxic waste to be removed from the brain which could help treat or prevent *neurodegenerative* diseases like Alzheimer's and Parkinson's diseases.

- It causes the loss of all symptoms of inflammation, such as fatigue, brain fog, fatty liver, skin blemishes, weight gain, high blood pressure, high cholesterol, type 2 diabetes, autoimmune diseases, depression, anxiety, etc.

- It decreases *immunosuppression,* the partial or total subduing of an individual's immune response, and death caused by chemotherapy. It also protects from *chemotoxicity*, (nausea, vomiting diarrhoea, mouth sores etc.) poisoning the body, or other harmful effects of chemotherapy. Fasting 36 hours before chemotherapy produces fewer side effects, and only cancer cells die.

Fasting Is Not for Everyone

Despite the benefits of fasting, some individuals, however, should avoid it. Always consult your doctor before fasting if you are on medication, have never fasted before, or are embarking on a long fast. Fasting is not recommended for children under the age of 18, pregnant or breastfeeding mothers, people who take insulin for type 1 diabetes, and people who are considered to be underweight and trying to gain weight.

Problems With Fasting

- **Hunger:** The hunger hormone, ghrelin, sets in soon after a meal is missed. Drinking water will help make one feel less hungry.

- **Headache:** This is due to dehydration or low blood sugar. Staying well hydrated with calorie-free beverages, plus maintaining stable blood sugar levels by eating a balanced diet before starting to fast, will help to prevent that.

- **Nausea and vomiting:** With regard to medication, some medications need to be taken with food; otherwise, nausea, stomach irritation, and vomiting may result. If you are taking medication, consult your doctor before you decide to fast.

- **Constipation:** Time-restricted eating, as well as dehydration, can cause constipation. Fasting for shorter periods, preferably alternate-day fasting should help prevent that, as well as drinking lots of water during the fasting period.

- **Insomnia:** Sleeplessness can also occur during fasting. This is because cortisol, the stress hormone levels, increases with hunger. This suppresses the production of melatonin, the hormone needed to fall and stay asleep. Exercising and staying active during the fast should make it easier to fall asleep. The fast should not be broken too late at night. At least 3 to 4 hours before bedtime will help sleep better.

- **Heartburn:** This may also be experienced during fasting since stomach acid is reduced due to lack of food. Stomach acid helps destroy bacteria, break down, and digest food. Avoiding high-fat and spicy foods when breaking the fast should help with heartburn during fasting. Also, avoid lying down on your back immediately after breaking the fast, thus enabling stomach acid to flow into the oesophagus, causing the burning sensation.

- **Electrolyte imbalance:** Fasting for more than 8 hours causes the loss of electrolytes; sodium, magnesium, and potassium since the need for electrolytes cannot be met through food. Staying hydrated is important during long fasts. Drink lots of calorie-free electrolyte water. This is available from grocery stores and pharmacies. Consuming this water will help to prevent electrolyte imbalance, which could lead to dehydration, fatigue, headache, dizziness, and palpitations during fasting.

Breaking A Fast Prematurely

In order for the fast not to be broken prematurely if it is not a dry fast, it is important to avoid sugar, sweeteners, and other calorific beverages, which could break the fast by causing insulin spikes. In addition to plain water, sparkling water, lemon water, black, unsweetened tea or coffee, green tea, and zero-calorie herbal infusions can be consumed without breaking the fast. Bone broth and collagen both contain calories and should be avoided.

Some multivitamin and other dietary supplements could also break the fast as they contain natural or artificial sweeteners, gelatine, collagen, and other calorific ingredients.

Fat-soluble vitamins A, D, E, and K should only be taken with food to enable better absorption. They should therefore be taken after breaking the fast.

With regard to medications that need to be taken on an empty stomach, if the medication is free from sugar or sweeteners and contains no calories, it could be taken during the fast. Otherwise, it could break the fast.

Fasting is so beneficial that I recommend it be done routinely and periodically by all healthy adults, with the exception of those listed above. Do consult your doctor first and, if necessary, fast under supervision, especially if you are on medication or going on a long fast.

Chapter 10

Slow Down The Ageing Process!

"Ageing is a fact of life. Looking your age is not."

— Howard Murad MD

Ageing is a cycle of life, a natural process whereby the body undergoes changes over time and continues to do so for the rest of our lives. It's an inevitable part of existence, as all living things grow old and eventually die. This is because cells gradually lose their ability to replace themselves over the years. Additionally, some cells, like red and white blood cells, have very short life spans. On the contrary others, such as those found in the heart, brain, and muscles, have longer life spans.

While chronological ageing is a natural process, premature or biological ageing is when it happens sooner than expected, resulting in the body appearing older than its actual age. This accelerated ageing is influenced by various factors such as genetics, diet, lifestyle, and environmental conditions. Our genes, dietary habits, physical activity, sleep patterns, stress levels, exposure to harmful toxins, and other lifestyle factors determine how early the process begins and how rapidly it progresses.

Signs Of Ageing

1. **Skin:** The skin becomes dull, dry, and wrinkled because the body produces less natural oils, or sebum as we age. The appearance of age spots, also known as liver

or dark spots, due to exposure to too much sun for decades. This leads to the overproduction of *melanin,* a pigment in the skin, hair, and iris of the eye, causing patchy discolouration spots, *hyperpigmentation.* Finally, it loses its elasticity and begins to sag due to damage caused to fibres in the skin, known as *elastin.*

2. **Hair:** The hair follicle cells lose pigment and start to turn grey. Additionally, hair becomes thin and begins to fall off owing to the death of the stem cells that trigger new hair growth in hair follicles.

3. **Joints:** The joints start to ache due to the erosion and thinning of the cartilage within the joint, making movement very difficult.

4. **Loss of muscle mass:** This is due to lack of physical activity, inadequate nutrition, and low hormone levels. Muscle mass and its function start to decrease, making it difficult to perform daily activities.

5. **Forgetfulness:** As we age, it is normal to forget things once in a while. However, serious memory loss could be a sign of the onset of cognitive decline, in which case a doctor should be consulted.

6. **Loss of sight and hearing:** This happens due to genetics, disease, and environmental toxins.

7. **Loss of bone density:** With age, bones lose mineral density due to poor nutrition, lack of physical activity, and a vitamin D deficiency. This causes the bones to become weak and more likely to break, a condition known as *osteoporosis.*

Factors That Contribute To Premature Ageing

- **DNA:** DNA damage due to oxidation and other factors can lead to *apoptosis* or cell death. Excessive apoptosis may eventually lead to neurodegenerative diseases like Parkinson's, Alzheimer's, and Huntington's diseases.

- **Poor diet:** A diet high in sugar and refined carbohydrates damages the skin's ability to produce collagen and elastin, thus causing skin to wrinkle and sag. It also results in higher blood sugar levels, which accelerates the ageing process.

- **Poor sleep:** Not getting enough sleep also accelerates the ageing process. The body repairs the damage that occurs throughout the day during sleep. It is during sleep that cell repair and other bodily processes take place. The American Academy of Sleep Medicine recommends that adults have 7-8 hours of sleep. Sleep is necessary to maintain healthy skin, not getting enough will only add more years to your age.

- **Dehydration:** Lack of hydration makes one prone to premature ageing and at risk for chronic diseases, such as heart and lung diseases, and early death, which is not the case for those who are well-hydrated. Dehydration also causes dry, rough, and itchy skin, which leads to wrinkles and sagging skin.

- **Smoking:** Smoking can also cause dry skin and wrinkles. This happens because smoking reduces blood flow, which makes it harder for the body to get vital nutrients for smooth and elastic skin.

- **Alcohol:** Drinking too much alcohol could lead to dehydration and cause the skin to lose moisture, leading to dry skin and wrinkles. It can also cause the brain to age, leading to alcohol-related brain damage and dementia, as well as fatty liver disease and *cirrhosis* of the liver, causing permanent liver damage.

- **Environmental pollutants:** Air pollution, ultraviolet rays, temperature, and humidity all subject the skin barrier to toxins and free radicals, causing loss of antioxidants, which make the *dermis,* (the inner layer of the two main layers of the skin) weak, thus adding years to your skin and increasing the risk for skin cancer.

- **Hormonal imbalance:** Hormone production decreases with age. The hormone oestrogen declines as women age, causing dry skin and leading to fine lines and wrinkles. It also causes low collagen levels, which results in thinning skin. Progesterone, which balances oestrogen levels, also decreases, causing the skin to lose hydration, firmness, and elasticity. There is also a decline in the male hormone testosterone, causing reduced mobility, and other symptoms such as reduced sexual function, reduced libido, and inability to sleep.

- **Chronic stress:** A study published in Cell Metabolism revealed that stress increases biological age, but that can be reversed with recovery from stress. Chronic stress, if not managed, causes the release of cortisol and adrenaline, stress hormones that can cause inflammation and damage DNA. DNA damage for long periods can also lead to oxidative stress, causing damage to cells and thus leading to premature ageing.

- **Inflammation:** Short-term inflammation is necessary for healing and repair of tissues. However, when it becomes chronic, it could damage healthy cells, tissues, and organs, and cause damage to DNA, which leads to premature ageing. It can also lead to neurodegenerative diseases like Alzheimer's disease and others.

Foods That Slow Down The Ageing Process

Avoiding junk food and eating only foods rich in antioxidants, vitamins, and other nutrients, as well as foods that are anti-inflammatory, may slow down the ageing process. Below is a list of some of the top nutrient-dense foods that will nourish the cells, keep them active, slow down ageing, and prevent age-related diseases.

1. **Berries:** Berries, especially blueberries, are the natural destroyers of free radicals that damage DNA and cause premature ageing. They are very rich in *phytochemicals*, which prevent cell and tissue damage, plus vitamins A, B, and C. In the case of blueberries, *anthocyanin* (a chemical that gives them the deep bluish colour) has antioxidant as well as antimicrobial properties. Anthocyanins fight free radicals and reduce oxidative stress, thus slowing down the ageing process. They also improve skin damage caused by sun exposure, prevent chronic diseases, boost memory, protect the brain against ageing, and slow down cancer growth. Blueberries, blackberries, raspberries, blackcurrants, and other dark berries are all rich in anthocyanin and should form part of an anti-ageing diet.

2. **Nuts:** Almonds, cashews, pecans, pistachios, and walnuts are all rich in vitamins, antioxidants, minerals, and omega-3 fatty acids, which prevent ageing and age-related diseases like heart disease, stroke, and some cancers. The protein, healthy fats, and vitamin E in nuts protect the skin from sun damage from UV rays, as well as prevent moisture loss, keeping it supple, thus preventing wrinkles, sunburn, and even skin cancer.

3. **Fatty fish and fish oil:** Wild-caught salmon and other wild-caught fatty fish such as herring, mackerel, sardine, and tuna are all rich in omega-3 fatty acids and have lots of health benefits for the body inside and outside when it comes to ageing. Omega-3 fatty acids help with oil production, which diminishes with age, thus preventing dry and sagging skin. They also protect the skin against damage from UV rays; help fight inflammation, and lower cortisol, both of which speed up the ageing process. Salmon, crab, krill, lobster, and shrimp all contain the powerful antioxidant *astaxanthin*, which reduces the risk of cardiovascular disease, dementia, and age-related vision loss and even prevents prostate cancer. It helps maintain skin's elasticity, making it smooth and free of wrinkles and fine lines. Eating at least two servings of fatty fish per week or taking a non-synthetic fish

oil, like krill oil supplement daily, will help take years off your skin and prevent age-related chronic diseases. It will also help ease joint pain and stiffness that affect mobility in seniors.

4. **Cruciferous vegetables:** Broccoli and Brussels sprouts are packed with vitamins, minerals, and *sulforaphane,* a natural plant compound that has antioxidant, antimicrobial, and anti-inflammatory properties. It repairs the skin, makes it glow, and protects against UV damage. Secondly, it decreases the level of *dihydrotestosterone* DHT, the hormone that represses hair growth, in the blood, thus reversing and putting a stop to hair loss. Lastly, it fights cellular inflammation, which is the cause of chronic diseases.

5. **Extra Virgin Olive Oil:** Pure extra virgin oil, which has undergone very little processing, is rich in vitamins A and E, antioxidants, *hydroxytyrosol,* an organic compound, and polyphenols. In addition to its culinary uses, it can also be used on the skin, hair, nails, and cuticles. It prevents skin from ageing and makes a great moisturiser, which is easily absorbed into the skin and leaves no residue. It calms redness, soothes the skin, reduces skin irritation, and protects it from sun damage, thus preventing wrinkles and fine lines. It also makes an ideal make-up remover that is free of chemicals.

6. **Raw cacao:** This is very rich in minerals, particularly magnesium, polyphenols, *theobromine,* and antioxidants such as *procyanidins,* that reduce damage caused by free radicals, thus slowing down the ageing process as well as delaying the effects of diseases that come with ageing. Cacao helps to protect the skin from premature ageing by improving the skin's moisture and skin tone and by calming redness and blemishes. It improves collagen production to help skin's elasticity and firmness. It also protects the skin from UV damage.

7. **Green Tea:** Green tea contains polyphenols and antioxidants, including *epigallocatechin-3-gallate,* a catechin known for its many health benefits. With

ageing, it protects the skin from free radicals that cause the skin to age and reduces inflammation. It helps fight DNA damage caused by UV rays. It contains vitamin C, which boosts collagen and maintains healthy skin. Finally, it helps prevent wrinkles.

8. **Pomegranate:** This fruit contains molecules that are transformed by intestinal bacteria into a compound, *urolithin*, in the gut, which helps muscle cells to protect themselves from ageing.

9. **Turmeric:** Curcumin, the chemical compound found in this spice, has antioxidant and anti-inflammatory properties. It is known to prevent and also repair damage caused to DNA. It also delays the symptoms of ageing as well as delays the progression of age-related diseases.

10. **Red wine:** The polyphenol, *resveratrol*, found in the skin of red grapes, as well as flavonoids like tannin, and anthocyanin, in the red wine, have antioxidant properties that protect the body against the free radicals that cause premature ageing and restore the skin's elasticity. Red wine also contains *alpha hydroxy acids* (AHAs), which are natural acids that have antiseptic and anti-inflammatory properties, reducing excess oil production, and preventing acne when applied directly to the skin. It also contains amino acids that help renew skin cells, and prevent sun damage, by providing a protective barrier for the skin. The antioxidants in red wine also cause skin to glow when applied to the skin. Lastly, red wine can be used as a facial toner, tightening the pores and improving the skin's complexion.

Self-Care Practices To Slow Down Ageing

In addition to following a healthy diet, taking proper care of the skin, as well as other self-care practices, are necessary to prevent premature ageing from the inside out. Below is a list of some basic steps to take to help decelerate the process.

- **Sunscreen:** Applying sunscreen daily is a must to protect the skin from harmful UV rays, which accelerate the ageing process. Always make sure to get organic or sunscreen products without toxic ingredients like formaldehyde, benzophenone, retinyl palmitate, avobenzone, etc. Safer options, according to the EWG, are mineral-based sunscreens with zinc oxide or titanium dioxide.

- **Exfoliation:** This sloughs off dead skin cells from the skin's surface. As we grow older, the body's ability to exfoliate slows down, leaving the skin dull. Regular exfoliation helps to clear clogged pores, prevents acne breakouts, and produces oil to get rid of dull, dry skin, leaving it soft, smooth, and with a nice glow. It also helps with the production of collagen and elastin, thus improving the skin's texture, delaying wrinkles, and slowing down ageing. Finally, it stimulates blood flow, improving circulation, which ensures that skin cells receive vital nutrients needed to be healthy.

- **Sleep:** Getting enough sleep (7-8 hours for adults) will help slow down the ageing process. It is during sleep that collagen production is renewed in order to maintain the skin's elasticity and prevent sagging skin. Secondly, during sleep, human growth hormone is released, which helps cell and tissue repair, causing the body to look younger. Finally, sleep deprivation can make the cells age faster and add years to your skin.

- **Exercise:** Research shows that regular physical activity can help fight the ageing process from the inside out. It helps build strong muscles and boosts bone health. It reduces the risk of chronic age-related diseases. It can also help decrease the appearance of loose and sagging skin. Exercise can prevent DNA damage, which is the number one cause of premature ageing. Finally, exercising the brain helps prevent cognitive decline. Crossword puzzles, word games, reading, and learning new skills help boost brain function, sharpen memory, make it easier to focus, and reduce the risk of neurodegenerative diseases.

- **Dietary supplements:** As we grow older, it becomes more difficult to absorb nutrients from our food, leading to deficiencies that can negatively impact our health. It is very important for older adults to take vitamin supplements to avoid nutrient deficiencies. One such crucial vitamin is B12, which promotes healthy cell growth and helps to reduce visible signs of ageing on the skin. In addition to healthy skin, it also supports healthy hair and nails. It makes the skin radiant and helps diminish age spots. It may also prevent premature greying of the hair. Another vitamin that helps slow down ageing is vitamin C. It helps boost the production of collagen, the absence of which makes the skin lose its elasticity and become prone to wrinkles. Being an antioxidant, vitamin C also neutralises the free radicals that cause oxidative stress, making skin look old and dull. Plus, it boosts the production of nutrients that restore youthful-looking skin.

Coenzyme Q10 or CoQ10 or Ubiquinol is an antioxidant produced naturally by the body and used by cells for growth and maintenance. It also neutralises free radicals that cause oxidative stress and may reduce the damage they cause. It protects cells from harm and slows down the progression of age-related diseases. As we grow older, levels of this enzyme decrease. COQ10 supplementation is recommended to improve heart health, high cholesterol, high blood pressure, diabetes, and other age-related diseases. Consult your doctor before taking this supplement, especially if you are taking blood thinning medication.

- **Stress Management:** Prolonged chronic stress, if not properly managed, may lead to high levels of cortisol, which leads to free radicals causing oxidative stress, which is the cause of premature ageing. Managing chronic stress is also necessary to slow down ageing.

A Lesson From The Blue Zones

To conclude this chapter on slowing down ageing, I would like to briefly mention the Blue Zones and what we can learn from their simple lifestyle of health and longevity.

The 'Blue Zones' was discovered by an American, Dan Buettner, in collaboration with National Geographic and some of the world's best longevity researchers. They are areas where people live demographically longer with the highest life expectancy, reaching up to age 100 and beyond. BLUE ZONES is now a brand and a registered trademark. There is currently a Netflix docuseries, "Live to 100: Secrets of the Blue Zones." I recommend watching the series if you have access to Netflix.

The Blue Zones have been identified as follows:

- **First blue zone:** The island of Sardinia, about 200 miles off the coast of Italy. It is believed that the highest percentage of male centenarians lives here and still rides bikes even at age 102. The men are mostly shepherds and move around quite a lot. They eat mainly unleavened bread made from wheat germ with cheese made from grass-fed goat milk, very high in omega-3 fatty acids. They drink homemade wine with the highest concentration of polyphenols. They grow their own food and raise animals, mostly pigs for meat.

- **Second blue zone:** The island of Okinawa, 800 miles south of Tokyo, Japan. Over here, they live for a very long time and tend to die in their sleep. Their diet is mostly plant-based; as a result, they have lower rates of cancer and cardiovascular disease. In Okinawa, there is no word for retirement. It simply does not exist.

- **Third blue zone:** America's blue zone is the Seventh Day Adventist community in Loma Linda, California. Adventist men live about 11 years longer than the average American. Their diet is strictly plant-based; they eat legumes, seeds, and green plants. The Sabbath is from sunset on Friday to sunset on Saturday. On Saturday mornings, they focus on God by attending service. Afternoons are devoted to social networks, while evenings are for taking nature walks.

- **Fourth blue zone:** Nicoya Peninsula in Costa Rica. They have the most beautiful beaches, eat a plant-based diet, and exercise daily, living very happy lives up to age 100 and above.

- **Fifth blue zone:** Ikaria, about 25 to 30 miles off the Coast of Turkey. More than 30% of the population live well into their 90s, and many even reach up to 100 without any chronic health problems. They live in tune with nature, eating only a plant-based diet. They get lots of exercise from working in the vineyards and olive groves.

According to medical researchers, anthropologists, epidemiologists, and demographers who studied the blue zones, they found the following nine lifestyle habits which all of them have in common.

- They move naturally. They do not sweat it out in gyms with any sophisticated equipment. They work on farms and do not have any of the labour-saving devices that we have in this part of the world.

- They have a purpose. According to research, knowing one's sense of purpose adds up to seven years of extra life expectancy to one's life.

- They experience stress just like all of us, but it is how they deal with stress that makes the difference. Religious beliefs and practices, as they do in Okinawa, taking naps in Ikaria, happy hour; enjoying homemade wine with friends in Sardinia, and prayers in the Seventh Day Adventist community of Loma Linda, California, is how they manage stress in order to avoid chronic inflammation which causes age related-diseases

- The 80% rule. "Hara hachi bu," as they say before a meal in Okinawa, means to stop eating when their stomachs are 80% full. It is interesting to note that in the blue zones, their dinner is the smallest meal of the day and is eaten in the late afternoon or early evening, and that's it for the day. They eat breakfast like a king, lunch like a prince, and dinner like a pauper.

- Plant-based diet. The diet of the blue zones is mostly plant-based. They eat more beans than meat, which is mostly pork and is eaten only 5 times a month, in very small quantities, about 4 oz per serving. In Loma Linda, many people are either vegan or vegetarian and eat no meat at all. Nuts are their preferred snack, just about a handful a day, at least 5 times a week.

- Alcohol (wine). Apart from the Adventists, people in the blue zones drink homemade red wine regularly but in moderation, 1 to 2 glasses a day with food.

- Part of a faith-based community. Most of the people in the blue zones are people of faith and attend services about 4 times a month. This act of attending faith services regularly is believed to add 4 to 14 years to life expectancy.

- Family first. In the Blue Zones, they put family first. Ageing family members are kept at home with the rest of the family or nearby. There are neither seniors' residences nor retirement homes in the Blue Zones. Keeping grandparents nearby is good for the children. Children living close to their grandparents tend to have lower mortality rates since they receive lots of love from them. Their relationships last a lifetime. They spend time with their children, who in turn care for them in their old age. This commitment to family is believed to add three extra years of life expectancy.

- Social networks. Hanging out with groups of friends who are committed to each other and have lived for long is contagious and helps to cultivate healthy behaviours. Also, studies have shown that people who have a strong sense of community and have healthy relationships with their family and community have good physical and mental health and live longer.

The people in the Blue Zones do not do anything extraordinary in order to live healthy and longer. They do not take pills or potions, nor do they get injections or go under the knife to maintain youthful looks. They just move naturally, grow and prepare their own food, not processed foods, eat more plant-based foods than animal products, pray and meditate or take naps to de-stress, have a purpose in life, and maintain a strong sense of community.

These simple tips from the Blue Zones, for a healthy lifestyle, should be a valuable lesson for us all no matter our geographic location.

Conclusion

It has been my greatest pleasure writing this book as my way of reaching out to the suffering masses who cannot afford the services of a health coach to guide them in making the much-needed lifestyle changes. It is my hope that the reader will enjoy reading it and find the information very useful as they embark on the journey to becoming a healthier version of themselves. There is no need to be overwhelmed. "A journey of a thousand miles begins with a single step." Just start by taking baby steps and be consistent. After all, the bad habits were not acquired overnight, so don't expect miraculous results immediately. Set small and achievable goals, and celebrate every small victory as you go along.

I also hope that this book will clear any confusion regarding leading a healthy lifestyle. Even if you don't get much out of all the other chapters, just retaining the lessons learned from the Blue Zones in the final chapter should be enough to get you started on the right path. I believe I have made this book simple enough for all ages, and the whole book could be read from cover to cover within a day. The information in this book, however, is for educational purposes only. It should not be substituted for medical advice. Consult your healthcare provider if you have any problems.

Wishing you a very happy reading and have fun with it. Here's to health and longevity!

Yours in good health,

~ Shika

yourhealthinyourhands2018@gmail.com